ODYSSEO

The Great Adventure

ODYSSEO, The Great Adventure

ISBN: 978-2-9814401-1-2
ISBN: 978-2-9814401-0-5

Legal deposit – Bibliothèque et Archives nationales du Québec, 2014
Legal deposit – Library and Archives Canada, 2014

Published by

Cavalia Inc.
5100 Hutchison Street, Suite 300
Montréal, QC, Canada H2V 4A9

PRINTED IN CANADA - June 2016

ODYSSEO
The Great Adventure

Written by **Raôul Duguay**

A journey to dream

Cavalia's second creation, the *Odysseo* show, is a call to dream, to move beyond time and space, to travel toward the mystery of new horizons and unfamiliar cultures while drinking in the most breathtaking landscapes on Earth. To transcend reality and to invite contemplation of the human condition and the future of our planet, *Odysseo*'s creators tapped into the universal tool that powers evolution: imagination.

If humans, in their quest for knowledge and meaning, were able to conceive of travelling to the ends of the Earth, it was thanks to the horse, the very first means of travel. It is the horse that propelled humans out of prehistory and into history. A powerful, pure wonder of nature, this animal helped build bridges between cultures, fostered alliances between nations and, by crisscrossing the globe, was one of the key drivers of humanity's evolution.

While riding horses brought new dimensions to human freedom, humans have long held this animal prisoner. Today, secure in the respect given to it by the whole *Odysseo* team, the horse is presented as a companion. Through subtle communication, horse and rider become one, conveying the shared dream of harmony between the human and animal kingdoms. Travelling together, completely free, they ignite our imagination and carry us into a world of utter magic.

A living dream

Odysseo is a living tapestry
an invitation to a waking dream
to travel beyond the centuries
to cross borders, mountains, streams
and see our planet most extraordinary

It is human nature
to dream
to fly on the winds of adventure
within our imagination
to discover new horizons
imagining a world
of beauty, harmony and hope

It is human nature
to reach out
to unfamiliar cultures
and to share
with other nations
a common dream
of living peaceful and free

The author's hope

Head in the clouds to peer into the future and feet on the ground to make their vision a reality, authentic creators earn their living by dreaming, by giving people something to dream about, by creating another world within the one we know. *Odysseo* owes its existence to Normand Latourelle, a bright-eyed dreamer who was able to share his vision with a team of well-known and immensely talented creators.

In thinking about how to tell the remarkable story of *Odysseo*, a universally acclaimed work of art, the first word that came to my mind was *echo*. This book is therefore meant to be an echo of the equestrian multimedia show *Odysseo*. It is an echo of the thoughts and actions of the people who have made this show a marvellous reality.

As I know nothing of the equestrian world, I decided to give voice to the forty or so creators, artists and directors directly involved with bringing *Odysseo* to life. Most of the texts that make up the heart of this book are excerpts of answers to questions I asked those involved in *Odysseo*'s creation. Together, they offer a wonderfully nuanced glimpse behind the scenes.

I am deeply honoured that Normand Latourelle chose me to write this book. We have worked together on many projects over the years, beginning in the early 1980s. Under his guidance, I co-wrote with him the booklet for the multimedia show *Les Légendes fantastiques*. And, as an idea-person, researcher and documentalist, I helped develop the *Cavalia* and *Odysseo* shows. I also wrote most of the lyrics for the songs used in *Odysseo*. After attending a dozen or so performances, I still consider this multidisciplinary show to be a poetic work of art. It is thus through the eyes of a poet that I describe each scene of the show. At the end of each section, I add the comments I gathered from the creators, artists and directors involved in its conception. And, since he's the one who initiated and very closely followed the evolution of this astounding group teeming with creative imagination, my main source of information was Normand Latourelle, the show's production designer and artistic director.

My hope, as the author, is that those who read this book will perceive a living echo of the symbiosis between man and horse and the harmony between humans and nature. The images and texts in this book reveal the human values expressed in the show. A cultural crossroads, *Odysseo*, which was created with a great deal of passion and joy, is a hymn to creation and to freedom.

— Raôul Duguay

The horse as artist

Happiness

"*Odysseo*'s 67 horses are the show's true stars," says Normand Latourelle. "We consider them to be not only athletes, but artists. So we take time to make them happy, creating a stage that is a playground large enough for them to express themselves."

Mr. Latourelle adds: "Indeed, if you want happy horses, you need happy humans. And to get happy humans and happy horses, you have to take care of them."

Nobility

The horse is a noble domesticated animal, noble in the sense that it is not a predator, but a prey animal that fears anything unfamiliar. Normand explains the best way to approach a horse: "To keep from frightening a horse, you must make its acquaintance very slowly and gently. Because, at first sight, the horse will view you as a predator. When it understands that you aren't a threat, it can become your friend. A horse will only approach you if it feels perfectly safe."

In Normand Latourelle's eyes, the horse is the most noble of the beasts. "I never met a horse that intended harm. In nature, the horse is prey, and flight is its only defence and means of escaping aggression. That gives it its nobility. It's rare for horses to seek revenge or attack a human. They'll only do so if they are mechanically restrained or physically cornered. But, generally, fighting isn't in their nature or culture. They're noble because when a human tries to engage in a power struggle with a horse, the horse's instinct is to flee. Force breeds force; violence breeds violence. What humans need to offer this animal is an equal partnership, a relationship in which the horse doesn't feel dominated. Horses agree to have a human on their back. They can read their rider's thoughts. Our own nobility calls us to do the same and give them as much freedom as possible."

For millennia, the horse has travelled far and wide, covering incredible distances. It is the animal that inspired humans to break out of their corner of the world, to visit other lands and discover and contemplate the wonders of nature and culture. It is thanks to the horse that we were able to explore the farthest reaches of our planet.

Odysseo, the show

The word *odyssey* opens wide the door to dreams. In the *Odysseo* show, all of the scenes that play out before our eyes are vivid dreams that invite us to embark on a fabulous voyage.

From mountain peaks to rolling sand dunes, from grassy plains to caves dripping with icy stalactites, from the mists of enchanted forests to dancing northern lights, from the Milky Way to lush pastures where man and horse sleep peacefully side by side, *Odysseo* takes us on a journey through the beauty of nature.

Odysseo is first and foremost an authentic meeting of man and horse. Based on consideration of the horse's needs, understanding of its behaviour and animal nature and respect for its freedom, this relationship has opened a true channel of communication between two species. It is the profoundly humanistic approach taken by *Odysseo*'s creators, trainers and riders that allow these two species to walk, run and travel together in this larger-than-life show that pushes the limits of all that is possible.

Welcome to the magic of this incredible odyssey. Enjoy the journey!

The Herd

*Is that the sound of angels? Celestial voices rise like
the morning mist, murmuring a sweet melody.
To the subtle sound of the guitar, we are plunged
into the mystery of an unfamiliar world. Silence falls
over the big top. The audience collectively holds
its breath.*

*How astonishing and delightful to discover horses
roaming calmly and freely, as they would in the wild!*

*The curtain opens. A woman emerges from
the shadow of the trees and approaches one of the
horses. She talks gently and strokes its neck.
According to mythology, the first human to tame
a horse was, in fact, a woman. With warmth and
welcome in her voice, she gives meaning to this
encounter by giving voice to her dream in song.*

Encounter

The voice of the wind
sings the song of a dream
of an odyssey
into eternity

The breath of the wind
sows the seeds of life
whose delights
fill our sights

Life is one long dream
and that dream is an odyssey
a voyage as free
as a water stream
an interior journey through the years
a quest to tame our fears
an expedition into adventure
to recover our true nature

To love life
to dream of freedom
to travel the Earth
with a peaceful heart

La voce del vento
racconta di un sogno
di libertà
di una odissea

Quel soffio di vento
afferra la vita
ti fa contemplare
questa eternità

La vita è un lungo sogno
e il sogno è una odissea
viaggio per la libertà
come I acqua scorrerà

Per vedere cio che sei
ritrovare cio che hai
curarti le ferite e poi
ritrovare la tua anima

Amo solo amo la vita
il sogno ama solo la vita
credo nel sogno l'amore la vita
io vivo nel sole e cerco l'amore

Lyrics by **Raôul Duguay**. Italian adaptation by **Fabrizio Voghera**.

In a very poetic, very intimate setting, men walk slowly out of the forest and approach the horses, who do not attempt to flee. Curious, the men make the acquaintance of these beautiful beasts, speaking to them, petting them and playing games.

Suddenly, a horse and rider burst out of the forest. The high-spirited mount wears no saddle, no bridle and no bit in its mouth. The rider races around, leading the woman, men and horses in a joyous whirlwind before inviting them to follow him out of the clearing. Where is he taking them?

From the very first moments, *Odysseo*'s message is easy to grasp. It is the harmonious meeting of and interaction between two species, humans and animals, each seeking to understand the other. Production designer and artistic director Normand Latourelle, who guided each step of show, explains his intention in this opening scene: "The idea behind this first scene was inspired by the relationship between man and horse."

Normand Latourelle knew that the show should open on horses roaming freely in nature. The humbly-dressed men approach the horses with the intention of taming them, of becoming friends. When they gather in the centre, the horses move toward them because they want to and because they trust the humans. This is a very touching moment. Once trust has been established, the horses appear to give the humans permission to climb onto their bare backs.

Says stage director Wayne Fowkes: "*Odysseo*'s opening scene is very poetic. We start by trying to understand the horse, presenting the animals in their natural habitat. Then, we wanted to show humans discovering the horse. In the relationship between these two species, our first connection is integration with nature. Our intention was to show how horses interact in the wild. In *Odysseo*, the two most important themes are travel and nature. They are the show's two main concepts: a voyage taken by humans and horses through the beauty of nature."

Set designer Guillaume Lord reveals his vision: "Nature is our main inspiration. We wanted the horses to be comfortable and happy onstage. To give them a feeling of freedom, we offered them a vast space."

The Fairies

The sky is dotted with pink and blue clouds. Six beautiful young female riders, each standing astride two white horses, stroll around the clearing. They look like fairies exploring a mysterious forest bathed in the bluish light of dawn. They guide their horses with one hand, the other jingling a cluster of small bells attached to their wrist. They are the epitome of grace and voluptuousness.

"In *Odysseo*, a few scenes make reference to universal symbols," explains the artistic director. "We're about to enter an imaginary world where fairies announce a voyage to enchanting horizons. The horses and the fairies with their little bells are like a call—a call to the imagination. This scene was technically challenging. With one hand, the riders have to hold the reins and guide their two horses. With the other hand, they have to sound the bells, whose ring is a call to the beyond, a call to the spirits. Ringing the bells is a very spiritual gesture, a ritual that encourages meditation."

The stage director explains what he wanted to create in this scene: "This is truly where the voyage begins, in this magical forest that returns us to a state of calm and innocence."

Catherine Mireault, *Odysseo*'s head costumer, says that to create this beautiful scene, the horses first had to get used to the riders' costumes. "A horse can be startled by the sight of a large piece of silk flying up. So the riders requested a piece of fabric to show the horses and get them used to seeing it. That's one of the things you have to keep in mind when using costumes around horses.

Village Celebration

In the heart of the forest, the staccato beat of African drums immerses us in the atmosphere of a village celebration.

Wearing dazzling smiles, a dozen Guinean acrobats enter the stage. With a fiery energy, they start a wild dance to express their emotions. Their intensity sparks joy in everyone watching.

Then, stilt walkers wearing springs on their feet (urban stilts) transform into human grasshoppers.

Horses and riders stream out of the forest and jump over horizontal poles. After each jump, the pole is set a little higher. Horse, human or stilt walker: who will jump the highest?

In this most festive scene, the director's intention was to show a competition between man, horse and mechanical man (stilt walker). "The acrobats jump, the horses jump higher and the mechanical men jump even higher. Getting the horses to do tricks is great, but here, beyond the competition, we designed a choreography that includes wonderfully humorous moments. This scene is a celebration of the joy of playing with horses."

As a child, Normand Latourelle often dreamed about the ability to defy gravity, to jump and fly higher than everyone else. In nature, horses love to run and jump. In celebration, *Odysseo* includes delightful moments showing acrobats and horses escaping the bounds of gravity.

Also in this scene, three acrobats on urban stilts astound the audience the moment they appear onstage. Learning to walk on stilts is not very difficult, but running, jumping and doing spins are extremely challenging. And performing perilous jumps forward and backward is quite a feat! "This act has unique challenges," explains acrobat Lucas Tormin Mendonca, originally from Brazil. "We jump quite high. And it's the first time ever that we perform on sand and in water."

Stilt walkers usually jump on concrete or grass. Learning to perform in water and on sand takes extensive training. While it took months to craft the perfect set of routines, *Odysseo*'s stilt walkers found the most effective techniques to ace this part of the show. This scene was inspired by the similarity between the shape of the stilts and the shape of the horses' legs.

Lucas is happy to say that respect for the horses has been the founding principle of the *Cavalia* and *Odysseo* shows. All of the artists who perform in *Odysseo* undoubtedly agree when he says, "The main reason I took this job was the humanistic approach to handling the horses. I told myself that if the *Odysseo* team treats its animals this well, it would treat the humans just as well and with the same amount of respect."

Freedom

Kneeling on a bed of moss in the middle of the clearing, her back to the audience, a woman, alone and completely still, appears to be meditating on the splendour of nature. Behind the forest, perched on the mountaintops, huge Easter Island statues watch the young woman discretely.

One by one, gorgeous snow-white Arabian stallions slowly approach her, circling around her. They seem to trust her completely. She rises and invites the horses to stand in line, turn around her, stop abruptly, dance and come closer. To reward them for their gentleness and generosity, she gives each a kind word and a caress.

Seeing a woman alone, with several horses moving freely around her and surrounding her, is to bear witness to a touching moment of genuine communication.

How does Élise Verdoncq, trainer of these young Arabian stallions, get them to understand what she wants? She revealed a few of her secrets to me: "Although I'm talking very softly, the horses understand me because, in this scene, the sound has been modified so that the horses can hear me, but not necessarily the audience. In this number, I'm in a harmonious relationship with my horses. We're there to play and have fun. Each horse recognizes his name. Because they were taught, they know their place, the order in which they need to move. They remember that they must be in first, third or eighth position. From the very start of our relationship, the horses read my body language. I move toward them or back up, I spread my hands or draw them together, I step closer to one horse than to another, and they understand all of that. With my voice and body language, I get them to perform a choreography. I want it to be lovely and flowing, not something routine. I try to add variety based on what the horses are prepared to give me. Afterward, we have to live with what works or doesn't. I always respect what the horses decide. They accept my requests because they want to. And they want to because they're free and we're having an exchange, we're sharing something in this playful moment. My role is to take note of whether or not everything we worked on was successful."

"And I don't want to cause any jealousy! By petting each horse that has done what I asked, I let them know that I'm there and that all is well because we're communicating in their comfort zone. My way of thanking the horses is to give them a gentle pat."

When I asked David Tardif-Latourelle, Vice-President of Market Development and Legal Affairs, what touched him the most in *Odysseo*, he answered: "The music is very moving. Michel Cusson, the composer, was able to capture the emotion in each scene and render it with a great deal of sensitivity. I also like the parts where everything stops, where we can emphasize what's happening onstage, for example, when we can hear the trainer speaking to her horses in the Freedom scenes. Since her whispers are barely audible, who would have thought that, under the world's largest big top, where 2 000 people are watching a one-of-a-kind show, the silence could be nearly complete? In this hush, something happens. There's a connection, a communication – if not a communion – between the woman and the horses. She speaks to them and they react immediately. We feel that they clearly understand what she's saying. They play the game with her. These small unexpected moments are the most moving for me. And in *Odysseo*, there are many such wonderful surprises."

Awed by the beauty of the relationship between the woman and her horses, composer Michel Cusson said: "Élise is a magician. It's as if she has a telepathic connection with the horses and these highly intelligent animals can express emotion. To reflect this lovely bond, I composed an airy classical melody that holds us suspended in the feeling arising from this very moving scene."

Odysseo's stage director told me that the scene brings us within. "I wanted someone to be observing the woman and her relationship with the horses. There is the audience, of course, but I also wanted something mysterious: the Easter Island statues. Their presence creates a sense of serenity, as in a ceremony. It's not easy to be understood by all of these animals. To succeed, Élise Verdoncq always remains calm. She doesn't order the horses to do things; instead, she encourages them by creating a peaceful moment. At every show, the audience wonders how such a bond can be possible."

According to Normand Latourelle, we are witnessing an authentic relationship. "Even though the space is vast and there are many horses, every interaction is gentle. The relationship between the young woman and the horses takes place in an atmosphere of subtlety and intimacy. To me, these Arabian horses are like ballerinas walking on tiptoe. I see them as graceful dancers."

Travellers

The big curtain slowly draws open, bringing the entire forest with it, as if by magic. Now we are in awe of the vastness of the space before us, in ecstasy over the splendour of such immensity.

A miracle takes place before our very eyes. On the horizon of this stunning stage, emerging slowly from an imaginary land, four splendid horses and riders appear on the crest of the mountains. They look like proud and noble princes and princesses, travelling by horseback from a kingdom where all is luxurious, calm and sensual.

Under a sky sprinkled with white clouds, the steeds and their riders, in all of their majesty and nobility, descend the mountain to the forestage. They are followed by a dozen other horses and riders. Crossing landscapes that are reminiscent of the Mongolian steppes, this mysterious caravan appears to be heading for an oasis, to drink in all manner of pleasures.

It is in this scene that production designer and artistic director Normand Latourelle's vision takes shape: "I got the idea for *Odysseo*'s set design when I was in the country. I was looking out a window and saw a wonderful sight: three horses in a meadow, suddenly appearing from behind a hill. That's when I knew we had to get the audience to admire not only the horses, but also nature. In *Odysseo*, the horses and the humans become companions that embark on an incredible journey through the wonders of nature. This scene is characterized by vivid colours. The riders' costumes are a feast for the eyes."

To bring Normand's vision to life, an immense stage – the largest in the world – had to be built, totalling 1,626 square metres (17,500 square feet). To form the 13-metre-high (43-foot-high) mountain, teams equipped with heavy machinery had to transport 15,000 metric tons (16,534 tons) of materials: a unique blend of sand, soil, gravel and stone. This mountain gives the show its grandeur and evokes the splendour of bucolic landscapes.

To allow the audience to discover the sheer size of the stage, and in order for the magic to work, set designer Guillaume Lord knew that they would have to play with the space. "To show how immense it is, we had to show only a small section first. When the show starts, we pull open the transparent tulle screen, behind which the audience can make out the horses entering the stage. But there is another curtain, on which we painted the forest that's used as a backdrop in the first three scenes. To get a full view of the stage, the forest has to disappear. And what magic trick do we use to make that happen? We simply pull open the large forest-curtain."

Once the forest disappears, we are faced with a set design that is absolutely grandiose. It is thanks to Quebec multimedia design firm Geodezik, specialized in creating and projecting 3D images, that Normand Latourelle's dreams became reality. We bathe in the luxuriance, the utter magnificence of the space. Our gaze is drawn to the mountain chains and the heavens. Everyone is blown away by such beauty. According to Étienne Cantin, designer at Geodezik, "3D video is an important aspect of several of *Odysseo*'s scenes. We had to create imposing landscapes that slowly change throughout the scene. The projected images are first drawn by hand, and then finalized on the computer. They are all original images."

In this scene, the costumes are especially majestic. Designed to cover the riders, but also partly their mounts, these costumes, with their discrete yet eye-catching hues, are attractive on both the male and female silhouettes. But designing this attire was not an easy process, explains Michèle Hamel, who co-designed the costumes with the late Georges Lévesque. "The only time the horses are costumed is in the Travellers scene. But in fact, it isn't the horses that are costumed, but the riders who are wearing a long robe that covers the horses' hindquarters. It was difficult to get the length right, so that the fabric wouldn't touch the horses' legs. Since each horse is a different height, the costumes had to be made to fit the horses' individual measurements."

Finally, Alain Lortie's lighting completes the picture. According to Normand Latourelle, "Alain is a genius with lights – a true artist. His work allows the audience to see the action onstage while admiring a vividly coloured, living painting."

Carosello

While northern lights dance in the sky, stars twinkle in shades of pink and red. Like horses roaming free, comets and shooting stars streak across the Milky Way. Mystery abounds.

Then something magical happens… In the quiet secrecy of the night, the forest reappears. Slowly, from the top of the tent, in the bluish half-light, wooden carousel horses descend toward centre stage. Seven princely riders come forward to greet this heavenly carousel, while an angelic voice sings praises to the Universe.

Carosello

The Universe is an illusion
an endless poem
whose verses conjure up
all the world's dreams

The sky is a carousel
of dancing stars
that light up the silence
like fireflies

The great wheel of life
turns, turns endlessly
Why do we lift our eyes
toward the light in the sky?

While galaxies flee
dreaming of infinity
we will also dream
and reinvent how we live

So long as the moon
circles the Earth
so long as the Earth
circles the sun
So long as the stars
make the Universe go round
We will turn ourselves around
and gravitate toward love

The great wheel of life
turns, turns endlessly
Why do we lift our eyes
toward the light in the sky?

Sing, sing of boundless love
sing the song of the stars
time freezes as it flies
space spins around
the great wheel of life
turns, endlessly turns

Why do we lift our eyes
toward the light in the sky?
To dream, to dream of infinity

L'universo è un'illusione
infinita poesia
dove i sogni in girotondo
accarezzano i pensieri e il mondo

Il cielo come un carosello
se le stelle danzano
brillano nel silenzio
come lucciole

Gira questa vita gira
ruota ancora senza fine
noi col naso in su a guardare
dove và a finire il cielo che và

Navigando le galassie
la paura di cadere
noi legati a questa vita
con la smania di cambiarla

Ma finchè la bella luna
farà il giro della terra
e finchè la nostra terra poi
sarà del sole come una sorella

Basterà una sola stella
per sognare ancora un pò l'universo è qui
nell'anima
noi giriamo su noi stessi e non ci
fermiamo mai
come gli angeli che ballano

Gira questa vita gira
ruota ancora senza fine
noi col naso in su a guardare
il grande sogno che vivra e non finira
non finira!

Gira questa vita gira
ruota ancora senza fine
noi col nas in su a guardare
il grande sogno che vivrà e non finirà

Canto l'infinito amore
di una stella il suo colore

Lyrics by **Raôul Duguay**, Italian adaptation by **Fabrizio Voghera**

What is most astounding about this mechanical carousel is the perfect timing of the movements performed by the aerial acrobats. The spectators are in awe of how the acrobats synchronize their movements to the rhythm of the music.

"Why use a mechanical carousel, with horses that aren't real?" I asked Normand Latourelle. He explains: "I couldn't help but reference my childhood. As children, many of us went to amusement parks that had a carousel. I remember imagining that the horses all around me were real. When it was time to get on, I had already picked a favourite horse. And if another kid had chosen the same horse, I wasn't happy. In *Odysseo*, the carousel is both realistic and imaginary. While carousels are usually painted dazzling colours, this one was left intentionally dark. It turns through the night and transports us in a dream. Movement is slowed down. And the song lyrics are a profound meditation on our place, as humans, in the Universe."

Elsie Morin and Mathieu Roy dreamed up the acrobatics and choreography in this magnificent scene. They also designed the rotating pole used by the acrobats.

Brennan Figari, one of the carousel's acrobats, had some surprising comments about this number: "Usually, we perform acrobatics on a Chinese pole. But in the *Carosello* scene, we perform dance moves on a rotating Chinese pole. Our movements are more graceful and fluid. In fact, we are performing a very subtle form of ballet, in which the synchronization with the other acrobats and the music needs to be very precise. Since the pole's rotation is computer-programmed, we must follow the rhythm exactly. At each performance, we respect the same rotation speed, whether slow or quick. You have to know exactly what to do and, when the speed picks up, be ready to adapt. Given that the poles and the carousel are turning simultaneously,

we acrobats are somewhat slaves to time. An acrobat who starts late will never catch up to the others, and the rest of the troupe will never catch up to an acrobat who started too early."

Darren Charles, Resident Artistic Director and Choreographer, makes sure that the movements are performed in unison. "If the audience notices that the aerial acrobats are not moving as one, that their movement aren't synchronized, they'll think that the act wasn't well choreographed. So it's my job to make sure the movements are perfectly timed with the music. To do so, we worked extensively with orchestra conductor Éric Auclair. As the music plays, the acrobats are given different signals. If they are late or early, the musicians end up catching up. But when everything goes well, it is the dancers who follow the music precisely."

The aim in this scene is to give the audience the impression that in our happiest dreams, our movements are slow and weightless.

55

Tribe

Now we are at the foot of ochre-red cliffs in a rocky, arid landscape reminiscent of the Arizona hills. It feels like we are on the set of a Hollywood Western.

Racing across the stage at full speed, cowboys play reckless games. Standing on their horse's hindquarters, jumping from one flank to the other, lying back in the saddle with both legs in the air, they take great pleasure in getting the spectators' jaws to drop, performing stunts that are as dangerous as they are daring. What a wonderful trick-riding demonstration!

To end this scene with flair, spirited riders arrive from all sides, carrying long red banners that float behind them. Are they announcing the departure of a united tribe, ready to ride off into the sunset in search of new wonders?

The spectators' dazzled eyes are riveted on this exuberant cavalcade. So ends the first part of the show: in jubilation.

"Energetic" is the word that best describes this scene. The audience is carried away by the joyousness that animates the horses and riders.

"Immense" is the second word that characterizes the sheer size of this playground, designed to allow the horses to cross the stage at a full gallop, manes and tails in a frothy cascade.

The more space they have, the freer the horses feel, as if they were out on the plains, and the more fun they have running full-out. Horses love to run. It is in this scene that these wind racers reach their top speed.

"Several techniques enable trick riders to move as one with the horse," explains Guennadi Touaev, Trick-Riding Trainer. "They aren't gymnasts performing acts on a stable pommel horse. In trick-riding, the horse is running at full tilt. The rider must carefully follow the horse's movements and rhythm to keep from throwing the horse off balance and to enable the animal to trust the rider completely."

The Odyssey

After the intermission, when the lights are turned down again, the audience suspects that something mysterious is taking place behind the large tulle screen.

The curtain opens on a breathtaking landscape, like a larger-than-life chiaroscuro painting... On the mountainside, 20 horses are stretched out on the ground. Men and women lie at their side, head resting on their horse's neck.

Day breaks and the sky turns azure. On the horizon, desert dunes undulate as far as the eye can see. So begins a long journey toward the unknown, an odyssey, a voyage taken in utter peacefulness and joy.

Dounya

Ah irafama	Ah! I adore you
Ah irafama dounya	Ah, Universe, I adore you!
Woula woula dalissé gbégbéna	In the forest, many animals
Wo meni nema	Take care of them
Yema yema dalissé gbégbéna	In the sea, other animals
Wo meni nema	Take care of them
N`na nouwama nanakhöma	My mother loves this world
Kiké to yambama Koremaya	It is full of beauty
Aboréwama nanaKhöma	The moon shines in the sky
Woula badè noun Guya to dalikhi	All our friends like to see
Moutanfan wamananakhöma	The forest, the sea, the mountains
Guérénama soya dounougnèma	No more war on Earth
Ah irafama dounya	Universe, I adore you!

Music and lyrics by **Yamoussa Bangoura**, Guinean acrobat, dancer and musician.

At the start of the show's second half, the audience is deeply moved by this scene demonstrating absolute trust between humans and horses. Faced with such a display of purity, truth and simplicity, one cannot help but admire the quality of the work put in by the show's creators and trainers, especially the subtlety of the incredibly nuanced staging, whose progression is simply brilliant. Wayne Fowkes is still surprised that they were able to make it happen. "Seeing 20 horses lying completely still and peaceful, their riders at their side, is a truly unusual sight. And there's something so poetic in that moment when the horses decide to get up."

Normand Latourelle's comment about the opening of *Odysseo*'s second half speaks to the philosophy espoused throughout the show. "We are witnessing a scene that is practically a miracle: 20 or so horses lying on the ground. We know that horses live mostly in silence. In the wild, this is to prevent predators from sneaking up on them. We wanted to start the second half of the show with a moment of total peace and happiness, with everyone listening to the sounds of nature."

The first of its kind, this act is quite an accomplishment. No one ever dared imagine that it would be possible to get 20 horses to lie on the ground at the same time. When the first horse gets up, it follows one of the performers. Then two, three, four horses join him, and in the end, there are over 32 horses and performers walking or running side by side.

This scene, a genuine dance of friendship, eloquently portrays the show's reason for being: the meeting and relationship of trust between the human and animal species.

Co-founder of the Cavalia company, Dominique Day, who helped develop this scene, describes its essence: "One cannot help but be profoundly moved, because something very real is taking place before our eyes. The horses lying down on the stage are not actors paid to play a role. It's their truth that they are offering. I have a feeling that this deep connection between humans and horses is what remains of an ancestral instinct, the strong desire to communicate with the other species in an effort to better understand it. And yet, no one has been able to pierce the mystery that is the horse."

Wayne Fowkes explains how he was able to stage this unique event: "I had discussed it at length with our equestrian director and choreographer. When we started training, only four horses would agree to lie down. I asked our leading trainers if it was possible to have 20 horses lie down at the same time. The entire team spent many hours training the horses to make it happen. It took a great deal of finesse, patience and energy to make this act a success. We wanted each rider to develop a subtle kinship, an authentic and enjoyable relationship with the horses. Here, we see the riders happy to run and walk with the animals. The better the relationship the dismounted riders and ground performers have with the horses, the easier it is to keep the show's unity and create choreographies that work well."

According to David Tardif-Latourelle: "This truly unprecedented number leaves all audiences in a state of contemplation. Those who know horses are amazed by the work it took to make this happen. Those who have not spent time with horses are moved by the authenticity of the relationship between the humans and horses."

The Storm

Suspended in midair during a fierce thunderstorm, spinning like tops,
two aerial acrobats, a man and a woman, balance precariously yet gracefully
in the blue-tinged air. A dozen other acrobats join them, invading the stage's
aerial space.

Suddenly, two young Arabian stallions who are fleeing the storm gallop around
the wind-buffeted acrobats. A lovely luminescent rain falls on the desert,
nourishing the arid soil. Blades of grass push out of the earth, greening the
plains as the African continent comes back to life.

In this hoop number, the stage director wanted to allude to the rainy season. At first the rain was simulated virtually, but then it was decided that actual water would fall at the end of the scene.

Aerial artist Brennan Figari, who literally flies through the air, defies gravity each day. "When I'm performing aerial acrobatics, I'm fighting gravity. But if I'm here now, it's because I can conquer it. When I'm in the air, my head clears. I concentrate on what I need to do and forget everything else."

"In my hoop, I'm sometimes 15 metres (50 feet) off the ground, with no net or harness. However, the technique remains the same no matter how high up I am. Performing at a height, in empty space, makes acrobats nervous. But the greater their experience, the more confidence they will have. In this number, one of the main difficulties is the speed at which I'm rotating. It's easier to perform a move when I'm not turning, so the faster I spin, the more challenging it becomes."

In some of the acts, it is vital to guarantee the safety of the performers. Running the many ropes, pulleys and motors used to operate all of the show's suspended components requires a watchful eye by the riggers. Brennan Figari explains: "Controlling the rise and descent of the hoop I'm using takes mathematical precision. When I'm performing my aerial choreography 15 metres (50 feet) off the ground, a highly experienced rigger must watch my every move. I motion with a hand or foot to let him know when to lift or lower me. We use the beat of the music to perfectly synchronize our movements."

A total of 173 different types of motors are used to lift and lower all of the components suspended to the ceiling of *Odysseo*'s gigantic big top, most likely a world record for a touring show.

The Call of Africa

Nature has awakened. The savannah is lush and green. Hundreds of birds flap their wings and take flight, making the sky shimmer. African acrobats play a pounding beat on the drums and dance with immense passion and energy. Moving to a frenzied rhythm, the dancers become acrobats, performing somersaults and pirouettes and jumping around like joyful gazelles. The crowd rejoices.

Normand Latourelle was very excited to discover these African artists. "After seeing videos of young Africans performing superb acrobatics for their fellow villagers on a beach in Guinea, I immediately became a huge fan of their contagious energy. These artists, who also dance and sing, are a very dynamic part of the show. It is extraordinary how versatile they are."

The *Odysseo* troupe now includes a dozen African performers. Their immense talent, dazzling smiles and joyous energy have a very positive effect on spectators, especially when they dance and invite the audience to sing along to "*Ô walou guere moufan*" (No more war on Earth). Everyone who sees them is spellbound by the ease with which they execute extraordinary movements and spins.

Composer Michel Cusson was very impressed: "Normand had mentioned hiring 10 exuberant Guinean dancers, acrobats and musicians. When I saw the energy with which they performed, it greatly influenced the music I was composing. It's when I listened to them play the *djembe*, the *kora* and the drums that my music took on a North African and Middle Eastern flavour. I combined African rhythms with other rhythms from around the world. In *Odysseo*'s score, the African culture's influence can always be distilled into one word: freedom."

This call for freedom can clearly be heard when Fode Ismael Sylla plays the *djembe*, or solo drum. Appointed by his fellow Guineans to be their spokesperson, he says: "We're all dancers, musicians and ground acrobats. We showed Darren Charles, the choreographer, what we were capable of doing. All of the dances, group acrobatics and choreographies were created based on his input, but he respected our way of doing things. Our dances are natural and inspired by our traditions. It's at school, in the streets and on the beach that we learned to dance, form human pyramids and perform stunning acrobatics. With my Guinean friends, it's incredible what we can do! On show days, we show up at the big top at 3:00 p.m. for our training session. We work very hard to develop and maintain our stability and flexibility because we need to be in peak physical condition to dance on sand and in water."

Darren Charles' experience with these performers has been very rewarding. "I came to work with the Guineans and, finally, prepared and choreographed all of the acrobats' scenes. I was inspired by their tribal dance, which they created together. I respected the way they moved, danced and sang. The more I got to know them, the better I could infuse elements of contemporary ballet, modern dance and jazz into their traditional African dances. Although it was difficult to keep them moving together and in sync, we finally created the perfect act. They really liked the way we combined acrobatics and African dance with the *djembe* and *dum dum* (big drum). It's a moment during the show in which they feel they are upholding their traditions."

«*Ô walou guere moufan!*»
"No more war on Earth!"

Paseo

Each standing atop their horse,
the fairies are wandering the mountainside.
We see what looks like a cave sculpted out of
a gigantic glacier. Long icicles, or stalactites,
hang from the ceiling. We enter a magical,
transparent place, an unexplored space of
captivating beauty.

The Angels

To the sound of ethereal music, four young women dressed all in white, each seated behind a rider on a white horse, approach centre stage like luminous angels. They suddenly unfurl their wings and fly into the sky. Their long, wide silks float gently around them. So elegant, so subtle, their aerial ballet inspires freedom.

Levitating over four white horses and their riders, these graceful angels perform arabesques and draw exquisite shapes in the sky. What rapture! In the cave, where all is cold as ice, a warm and tender voice sings a hymn to beauty and peace.

Angels

A few instants
of eternity
of liberty

A few instants
free of gravity
floating free

In the light
between Earth and sky
to dance wild
to wander
in nature
full of wonder

In lovers'
enchanted eyes
the stars still dream
of shining

From way up high
all is beauty
And peace flies
at the Universe's heart
All is joy and light
perfect joy

A few instants of eternity
in paradise
dazzled by beauty's
infinity

And to see at dawn
the sun blossoming
into the sky's
loveliest flower

Alone in space
surrounded by wonders
a heart full of thanksgiving
for the life that's awakening

No one can go higher
or further than their grandest
dream
to go, to go
in search of tomorrow

From a bird's eye
everything is lovely
Down on Earth
from the mountains to the seas
from the blues to the greens

Rooted
in Earth and sky
the tree, enchanted,
blossoms in the light

True pleasure
here and abroad
is found in this flower
housed in our hearts

To adventure
into nature
where the fondest dreams
nestled in our hearts
spread their wings
Under the sun
Life is amazing

Qualche momento d'eternità
di libertà
qualche momento senza età
sospeso là

Fra terra e cielo io e te balliano
un'avventura vita mia
mi sorprenderò

L'amore ha gli occhi impazziti stregati
le stelle ancora fanno innamorare

Tutto lassù è già bello così
la pace è luce nel cuore dentro me
tutto è sereno
tutto è sereno

Del paradiso la beltà io sognerò
tutti stupiti dall'idea che non finirà

L'alba ritrova il sole che riposa
che meraviglia il cielo al suo risveglio
per ringraziare da solo l'universo
per consolare la vita e il suo corpo

Tutto lassù è già bello così
la pace è luce nel cuore dentro me
tutto è sereno
tutto è sereno

L'anima in volo esulterà non morirà
come un uccello canterà s'innamorerà

Non ha radici e il cielo è la sua casa
l'albero abbraccia il suo
profondo sogno

Felicità sogno che vive
un fiore che è dentro di me

Qualche momento d'eternità
di libertà
qualche momento senza età
sospeso là

Tutto è sereno
tutto è sereno
tutto è sereno
tutto è sereno

Lyrics by **Raôul Duguay**. Italian adaptation by **Fabrizio Voghera**.

The audience is enraptured by such a sublime sight. The artistic director recalls how this scene came to be: "Inspired by Pegasus, the winged horse in Greek mythology, we wanted to incorporate flying horses. Of course, outside of fairy tales, horses cannot fly. To evoke the dream of flying, we worked with aerial acrobats. In this celestial ballet, the angels of our imagination fly above the horses and riders."

According to Japanese mythology, horses and riders have an angel that protects both at all times. The lovely choreography in The Angels scene was created by Alain Gauthier: "This scene holds us in a state of expansion. At first, we intended to use cables. Then, during rehearsals with the acrobats, we introduced the more poetic idea of replacing the cables with silks. To put on this number, the major technical challenge was to keep the rotation and handling of the silks constant while holding the horses at a synchronized, orderly pace. This adventure was very interactive. The communication between the artistic director, equestrian director, technical director, composer, lighting technician, riders and acrobats was very efficient. The result reflects the meeting of all these minds."

Nomads

The sun sets in the forest. Fireflies glow in the underbrush. Big drums sound in the distance.
Several hot-headed riders burst onto the scene. At breakneck speed, they take turns performing exhilarating
stunts on their mounts. Everyone is spellbound by the high-risk acrobatics. This adrenaline-fuelled scene
is an audience favourite.

Cossack trick-riding involves performing gymnastic and acrobatic acts on a horse that is not wearing a saddle, only a special surcingle (strap). An acrobatic demonstration on horseback, these perilous stunts require a good dose of daring, of course, but also perfect knowledge of the horse's behaviour. The act will not be a success if the rider, the *djighite*, has not earned the horse's complete trust. Regardless of what moves the trick rider is performing on the horse's back and the pressure he or she is exerting, the horse must continue to gallop, energetically and smoothly, in large, steady circles.

In this scene, Alain Lortie adjusts the lighting based on what is happening onstage: "When the Cossack trick rider passes under the horse's belly, the drummer beats to each of his movements. The spotlight shining on the rider must be as strong as the beat. The music has a considerable effect on the intensity of the lighting. You have to know when and how long to apply the effects. On the other hand, the music is also influenced by the acrobatics. In short, all are closely interconnected."

Guennadi Touaev, Cossack trick-riding trainer, must also adapt to the situation: "In the Cossack discipline, to keep the horse moving at the same pace, you have to always stay calm and respect its movements, otherwise it could lose its balance. The most important thing is to keep a cool head and trust your mount. Mutual trust makes things easier and more pleasant. If a rider doesn't trust his horse, he'll have a tendency to overly control its movements. When I'm trick-riding and respect my horse's rhythm, I don't get tired. I feel good and have fun. That takes time and experience."

In the *Cavalia* and *Odysseo* shows, a choice was made to forbid the use of spurs. Guennadi is very clear on the subject: "You should never force a horse to do something it's not prepared to do. Like people, horses have their own personality. We therefore have to work with each one individually. That being said, Cossack trick-riding is not for every horse. I prefer light, quick horses that are solid on the ground: American Quarter Horses. Lusitano and Spanish Purebred horses are more suited to the classical art of riding (*haute école*) and dressage."

The trick riders are not the only ones who have to adjust to the horses' pace. The musicians must also follow the action and note the horses' every move. Each performance is unique and alive. The horses do not necessarily always move the same way every time. Éric Auclair, who directs the live musicians, explains: "The Nomads scene, with its Cossack trick-riding, is action-packed. Once onstage, the rider performs his number after a first go-round, but sometimes he needs three turns and takes more or less time to perform that particular figure. In this type of scene, I have to adapt each time the rider passes. After hundreds of performances, I generally know what will happen onstage, but in an action scene like this one, there can be surprises. Of course, all the musicians know their parts by heart. They anticipate the decisions I'll make, because they're watching the same scene I am. If something unexpected happens, I have to quickly make a decision. But not too quickly, because everything might change between the time I give the signal and the musicians follow my lead. And if I'm too late, no one

has time to react. I need to wait for the right moment and act with assurance, giving a clear signal my musicians will understand so that the orchestra can immediately adapt to the situation."

For those who love a good Western, Cossack trick-riding is a crowd pleaser. Says stage director Wayne Fowkes: "In *Odysseo*, there are moments that bring us within. But for the show to flow, there also needs to be moments that are purely physical, where the performers can express their enthusiasm. Cossack trick-riding is edge-of-your-seat. It gets the heart racing and is fun to watch."

Everyone holds their breath when Clément Mesmin performs one of the most dangerous stunts in Cossack trick-riding: "When I pass under the horse's belly while it is galloping in a circle, the most difficult part is keeping my focus. There are three of us performing this trick each time: the horse, me and Guennadi. None of us can afford to make a mistake."

The Great Adventure

In the distance, immense waterfalls cascade down the mountains. Alone in the half-light, in the deep calm of the mountaintop, a female rider and her horse are practicing the classic art of dressage, performing figures filled with grace, dignity and majesty.

Meanwhile, on the plains below, something absolutely stunning is happening: Water is slowly covering the entire stage. Where is it coming from? Little by little, as if by magic, a lake forms at the foot of the mountain. No one can believe their eyes. Amazed, the audience gazes at the lake as it reflects the mountain.

Then, riders and horses begin an equestrian ballet in the water. Everyone is dazzled by the sight.

Suddenly, a dozen proud young Arabian horses stream into the lake. They seem to delight in running through the water, splashing the spectators in the first several rows and fully enjoying their freedom, as they would in nature.

Heeding the call, horses arrive from all directions to whole-heartedly join in the fun, racing and playing from mountain to lake and lake to mountain.

For this scene, it was a huge technical challenge to create a body of water large enough for the horses to play in. The lake that appears onstage is formed with a very efficient system that pumps water from two backstage tanks into a basin at astonishing speed. The same pumps remove the water at the end of the show. To create this moment of euphoria, both for the audience and the horses, 303,000 litres (80,044 gallons) of water are used and recycled. This last image of freedom in all of its splendour promises to capture the hearts of every audience member. The audience can observe that the horses of *Odysseo* (and *Cavalia*) are probably more liberated onstage than any animals in any show ever.

How did Élise Verdoncq, the rider of the Lusitano horse Omerio–this scene's big star– form such a lovely bond with her horse? She communicates through verbal cues and body language and not much else, in what she calls the Liberte style of horse training. She says : "The stage is really big and the horses are really free." Every interaction must take place within an authentic relationship and the focus must be entirely on the horse. There's no use fighting with the horses to make them obey. Everything must be done with gentleness. It's all so simple and logical that I wondered why I had never thought of it before. My body movements, a shift in weight, what I do with my legs and my hands will make the horse move in such and such a way. For example, to have Omerio perform the Spanish step, where he raises his leg high up and out, I apply a little pressure with a rein and then pressure with my opposite leg, by shifting my weight. The horse understands he has to raise his leg. I then ask him to do the same thing on the other side. He understands he has to raise the other leg and does so. My work with Omerio involves making him feel balanced, light and comfortable. He has to be free and able to feel the slightest movement of my body and legs. When he has understood, he docilely does as I ask."

Regarding this widely admired scene, Normand Latourelle reveals, for those who are familiar with the equestrian arts, the principles that all of the trainers and riders on his team must respect: "The *Cavalia* and *Odysseo* horses are the world's best treated. Respecting these magnificent animals is of utmost importance to the entire team. Are we perfect? No. Do we make mistakes? Of course. But I always make it a duty to remember that there's no room for impatience when working with horses. Horses don't make mistakes. It's the humans who don't understand them. I don't demand perfection from the horses. For example, in the Travellers scene, I accept that some have their head lowered and others have their head held high, or are looking to the right or left. In *Odysseo*, we don't tolerate the use of spurs. We use a gentle bit, called a snaffle. Only one horse has a rigid bit and that is Omerio, who performs the dressage and water tricks with Élise Verdoncq. The figures she asks him to perform are so refined that she has to be able to send him precise signals. But Élise is always very gentle. In short, we want the horses to keep their true nature."

Odysseo

On an immense screen, appearing from another world, seven huge
white virtual horses, emerging from the surf of a giant wave,
thunder toward the audience, carrying a tide full of new dreams.

In a spectacular final splash, the performers take turns parading
past: riders spinning in the water on their steeds, acrobats
turning in hoops high in the air, the dynamic African dancers
performing a series of perilous jumps, the stilt walkers hopping
and pirouetting in the water and the Cossack trick riders
galloping across the stage.

The entire sky is splashed by a giant wave. Millions of joyful
bubbles make the sky glitter. The performers bow before an
audience forever won over by their many talents. After every
performance, the spectators rise as one to give Odysseo a
standing ovation.

When the curtain closes, the audience appears to be satiated
by so much beauty. After their voyage through the wonders of
nature, they slowly file out of the big top and head home,
their heads and hearts filled with dreams.

Tuned in to the horses

A Passion for Horses

According to our trainers, the psychology of a horse requires a very delicate approach. The horse is a mirror. Attuned to its rider's breath, it feels everything and reflects back the rider's state of mind. If the horse is nervous, there's a good chance that the rider was nervous at the start of the session. Before asking a horse to do something, you must work on yourself, to become aware of the energy you bring to the horse.

The show's training philosophy involves teaching each horse to do a number of very different things. By exposing them to a larger number of disciplines, it is easier to keep them from getting bored. Also, if the horses are not always using the same muscles and joints, they will be able to better re-balance their bodies. For a show like *Odysseo*, you need horses that are in a positive frame of mind. The easiest way to understand their complex nature is to look deep into their eyes. A horse's eyes reveal how it is feeling. To ensure the horses' comfort and well-being, the quality of the time the horses and riders spend together is of utmost importance. Equestrian techniques can be taught, but love of – and passion for – horses cannot. Trainer Escalon said : "For us, it's not about technique as much as about feeling. When you see the horses on the huge stage, you see they are really expressing themselves."

Odysseo's trainers choreograph the horses' movements. Some may believe that choreography is simply a matter of technique, but according to our trainers, technique means nothing to a horse. Performing a double back salto has no value. A horse friendship is more valuable to them than performing the most amazing act in tense, stressful atmosphere or getting results through domination. They prefer being able to walk with a horse that they feel is fully with them, that isn't trying to flee.

Caring for the *Odysseo* horses is a group responsibility. There is no "my horse." There is only "the horses" and their well-being is everyone's business, even if certain members of the troupe are assigned specific tasks, such as feeding, grooming and getting the horses ready for work. This daily responsibility takes precedence over any other consideration, personal or collective.

Rules of Conduct

According to our trainers, if a rider wants a horse to do his or her bidding, a few rules need to be followed. First, never ask a horse to do something it is not physically capable of. Second, make sure that the horse has clearly understood what you are asking. Third, the horse must be interested in and enjoy doing what the rider or trainer is asking. This enjoyment often has to do with the human's state of being. If the horse senses that the rider is relaxed and able to enter into a friendly relationship, the horse will be soothed.

In their day-to-day lives, horses are always very fair, regardless of their personality or breed. This is because they are non-confrontational. If someone acts aggressively toward them, they will flee. Unlike humans, who demonstrate a lack of wisdom by pursuing confrontation, horses never engage in conflict. To become true partners, humans and horses cannot fear each other. To reach a better understanding, they must get to know one another.

For Ramon Molina-Gonzalez, rider and Equestrian Director on Tour, the horse represents strength, rapport and sharing. He believes that horses have authentic personalities and are always genuine in their relationships. Which is why he claims that the horses are the ones teaching the trainers and riders. "They're the ones who let us know what's fair or not. If I approach a horse while focused on my problems or in a bad mood, I won't be able to concentrate on our relationship. Since I'm preoccupied, it's impossible to create a moment of sharing. If the horse feels that I'm not fully present, it won't interact with me." The horse becomes the teacher when it feels truly at one with the rider. For example, on days when the rider is more tired, is less patient, asks a little more of the horse or forgets to listen to it, the horse will not respond to his demands. "You can only clearly feel a horse when you're actively listening. This requires constant self-work. And that's why horses are teachers without compare."

Training and Learning

Trainer and rider Élise Verdoncq freedom-trains the Arabian horses and teaches classic mounted dressage. The freedom training involves creating a scene in which the horses move freely around her. "It starts as a game and little by little, the choreography takes shape. As I spend time with them, I learn to decipher their body language. They respond to my voice and movements. What I find most gratifying is their trust in me. This develops when they feel truly comfortable around me. Horses are like children. And when I'm working with them, I feel like a kindergarten teacher."

A Day in the Life of an *Odysseo* Horse

Every day, each of the 67 *Odysseo* horses, all stallions or geldings, are carefully monitored, to see if they are eating well, drinking enough and are in good physical shape. The team makes sure that all of the horses performing in the show are healthy, and ready and willing to perform. About 20 people work in the stables year-round, making sure that the facilities are clean and pleasant for the equine occupants.

Nicolas Vandenplas, manager of the *Odysseo* stables, describes a day in the life of the horses on tour. "Their day begins at 7:00 a.m., at which point the morning staff have already started their chores: cleaning the box stalls and distributing hay and water. Our horses receive grain three times a day. It's an extruded feed, which means that it's cooked and easier to digest. Every morning, the horses also receive minerals and a vitamin A supplement."

Even when *Odysseo* is touring the United States, the hay the horses eat is shipped from Quebec. "I make sure they always eat the same type of hay. And they eat a lot! If we lined up the hay bales Cavalia uses in a year, it would be 100 kilometres (62 miles) long."

Due to their vulnerability to predators, like most large herbivores, horses only sleep three to five hours per day. In the animal kingdom, the horse is unique in one regard. By locking its legs, it can enter into a light sleep while standing up, dozing for 20 minutes or so at a time. Horses only enter deep sleep when they are lying down. And they snore, loudly. However, they will not lie down if their bedding is dirty or uncomfortable. Dominique Day, known by the entire team as the guardian of the horses' well-being, sees that the grooms prepare a big makeshift mattress by laying down a thick layer of light wood chips for each horse. Nestled in this ideal bedding, the horses sleep like royalty. But what they dream about, no one knows...

During the time it takes to dismantle the big top in one city and put it back up in the next, the horses vacation on a farm with lush green pastures, where they can bask in the sun and graze to their hearts' content.

People often wonder how they should approach a horse. Most put their hand on the horse's face, which they do not particularly enjoy. However, if they dislike it, they will simply turn their head. And if they do like it, they will stretch their head toward your hand. Generally, horses enjoy when you scratch their neck because it is a hard-to-reach spot. But not all horses are the same. Some like having their nostrils tickled, but not all!

While touring, one entire big top is used as a stable. The horses' coats are carefully brushed and rinsed before each show. A farrier, two equine health technicians and 20 grooms ensure that *Odysseo*'s stars are in perfect health. In order to have access to a veterinary hospital and any medication that may be required in an emergency, a licensed veterinarian is selected in each city.

To feel their best and enjoy some fresh air and sunlight, all of the horses are turned out into a paddock for at least an hour a day. This is a very important part of the routine, as it makes a difference later, onstage. In each city the show visits, Cavalia requires that there be sufficient room to set up outdoor enclosures.

The equestrian centre in Sutton

Cavalia's permanent equestrian facility is located in Sutton, in the province of Quebec, Canada, 10 kilometres (6.2 miles) north of the state of Vermont (U.S.A). In an indoor arena built specifically to prepare for the *Odysseo* show, an entire team spent over a year developing and testing original acts. In addition to pastureland, the centre includes two indoor arenas, three heated stables and Cavalia's administrative offices.

Dominique Day, who co-founded the Cavalia company with Normand Latourelle, keeps the equestrian centre running smoothly. "The centre is where we prepare new horses that we buy to take over from those that will be retiring. It's also a vacation spot for the horses. They can return here for several months, even years, before going back to work. Finally, horses that are no longer performing in the show come here to retire. We set aside significant sums and make considerable efforts to give our horses a good retirement. About 50 horses currently enjoy our 72-acre property, most of which is pasture. In keeping with our values, we feel that it's important to ensure the well-being of our horses at all stages of their lives, during their working years and after. About 20 people care for the horses at our equestrian centre in Sutton, which also serves as a testing ground for new training methods that ensure the well-being and serenity of working horses."

The Latourelle family

One of the most touching things about this wonderful family adventure that gave rise to the Cavalia company is the mutual admiration the team members have for one another. This attitude promises a prosperous future for this company, whose success and significant cultural contribution have been praised far and wide.

"Dominique, David and Mathieu support me and nurture my ideas. My sons are my best friends," says Normand Latourelle

Normand Latourelle

"Today, in addition to the success of the *Cavalia* and *Odysseo* shows, what brings me joy is to have my entire family involved in growing the company. Working with family is wonderful because you're with people who are like you, who understand you and are aiming for the same goal. We never fight. And I know that Cavalia has a bright future because young people are interested in the company's development."

The admiration expressed by the people who worked with Normand Latourelle on *Odysseo* may seem excessive, but what they say about the show's production designer and artistic director and the chairperson of Cavalia's board is sincere. Says stage director Wayne Fowkes: "To put on a show like *Odysseo*, you have to be a little nuts. Even to invest in such a project... Normand is brave, courageous and sincere. When he wants something, he'll do anything to make it happen. His energy drives him toward success."

Stage manager since 2007, Annick Gouaillier is not shy to say that "Normand Latourelle is *Cavalia* and *Odysseo*, followed by the creators who surround him and all of the teams. For us, it's a profession. For Normand, it's the dream of a lifetime. We're helping make his dream come true. His greatest achievement is never giving up."

Dominique Day

Dominique Day has been involved in the adventure from day one. In 1999, when the business was founded and the first show was being created, Dominique Day helped Normand Latourelle prepare his business plan. In addition to being co-founder and executive vice-president of the company, she played a major role in its communications and marketing department. It was she who made the wonderful discovery of the word *Cavalia*, in collaboration with the Cossette communications firm. This word has become both the brand of a thriving business solidly anchored in reality and the name of a show that invites people to dream. "I built our business brand year after year," she told me. "I did it while we were on tour the first four years. When we decided to base the marketing team at the head office, I continued to work remotely, from our equestrian centre in Sutton. Today, we can count on an excellent team, which allows me to spend more time on my passion for the horses and their well-being. But I continue to be involved in the marketing of the *Cavalia* and *Odysseo* shows, ensuring that our communications continue to represent our identity and values."

Dominique's involvement in Cavalia is directly tied to her love of horses. She is their advocate, seeing to it that everyone respects these magnificent animals. She makes sure that they are comfortable and never exploited. Her code of ethics is based on a solid set of values, a philosophy that promotes the well-being of the equine species. She believes that no human being on Earth has the right to benefit from or cause the suffering of any animal or fellow human.

Dominique now manages the Cavalia centre in Sutton, where she takes special care of the retired horses and those in preparation or training to become future stars in the company's shows.

Normand's two sons, Mathieu and David, share a cultural past that strengthens their bond, since they travelled similar paths. They grew up in a family in which the arts were a part of daily life. Everyone they knew either worked in show business, entertainment or communications.

In 2003, when the very first *Cavalia* shows were being performed in Shawinigan, Mathieu joined the team. He had been working on the trading floor of the Montréal Stock Exchange when his father invited him to help out in the family business by taking charge of concessions and merchandise, his first duties. Mathieu was actively involved in building the business, learning quickly and continuously. He went on tour, prepared *Cavalia*, then became executive producer of *Odysseo*.

"The Cavalia company is founded on a family and a rising generation," says Mathieu. "It will be fantastic when my nephew, nieces or my own children come on board. Working on building the Cavalia company and now the *Odysseo* show gives me a reason to jump out of bed in the morning because, of the many family businesses in the equestrian world, ours stands out. I can say with pride that I work for a company that makes people happy by offering them a beautiful dream."

Mathieu Tardif-Latourelle is always happy to go on tour. For him, being part of a great team and having the opportunity to travel give meaning to the tour, and working with family is what motivates him the most. Beyond business, he enjoys protecting the company's human side.

Busy managing various business aspects, Normand Latourelle decided to take charge of design and creation and let Mathieu deal with everything practical relating to the creation and production of the Cavalia shows. Mathieu therefore manages the budget, schedules, suppliers, hiring, human resources, staff training, supervision and everything incidental to creation. He is proud of what he does. "I found my niche, as a producer. Delighting people with a beautiful show is what I want to do with my life. Happily, Normand gives us, my brother David and I, plenty of leeway to build Cavalia's creations."

For nearly two years, Mathieu invested all of his time, energy and resources in the *Odysseo* project. "Working at Cavalia is an extraordinary experience. Since I'm captain of this ship, my role is to teach the business culture to all of the staff members and performers. Together – since this requires a vast amount of teamwork – we have reached our goal, to enchant people with a truly unique show, the only one of its kind in the world."

Then it was David's turn to contribute to Cavalia. In 2006, as the business was expanding, Normand suggested that his eldest son join the team as vice-president of market development and legal affairs. At the time, David was working as a lawyer in a prestigious Montréal law firm. Overnight, he made the decision that would change the course of his life. By morning, no doubt remained. He had to be part of this wonderful adventure.

Although stimulating, David's profession was never completely satisfying. "I studied law, but I always felt like something was missing. When I joined Cavalia, the emotion I got from the cultural aspect, the missing link, fulfilled me. Personally, being involved in Cavalia is pure pleasure. It's also a passion, a dream. Sharing this work with my family fills me with pride and the drive to continue. I learn a great deal from Normand. Our company sells emotion, first and foremost. Beyond the leading-edge technology, special effects, immense big top and the large number of horses and performers, everything we do comes down to one thing, the way we make the audience feel."

Few shows manage to convey power and emotion like *Odysseo*. It is both expansive and intimate, immense and infinitesimal, in the sense that it is a show of epic proportions, but also contains moments of great sensitivity and tenderness. The creators and performers do everything in their power to give audiences the best show possible, an attitude that ensures

the company's success. To put on a huge show like *Odysseo*, you need a remarkable team, to be able to support the show and ensure its continuity. "But you also need heart, and Normand, in his way of doing things, uses both his head and his heart. When you're in the stands, you don't get the feeling that the show was created according to a formula. Everything that happens is original, unique, interactive and real. *Odysseo* gives me adventure, discovery and the beauty of a dream that carries me to a universe that exists nowhere else on Earth," says David.

From his first days at Cavalia, David has managed the legal aspects of taking the shows on tour around the world. He also oversees the market development for the *Cavalia* and *Odysseo* shows. In the last 10 years *Cavalia* has been performed in over 70 cities and travelled half the globe. *Odysseo*, created in 2011, has the same bright future. "Having people experience the *Cavalia* and *Odysseo* shows on every continent is the dream of a lifetime," confides David.

Working alongside her spouse, David Tardif-Latourelle, Jo-Anne Martin contributes to the company as director in charge of developing the Cavalia brand. She manages the merchandise: items capturing special moments during the show, souvenirs, etc. For Jo-Anne, being on this great adventure with her spouse and their three children is pure bliss. "We're preparing the next generation to take the reins," she says with a smile.

Meet the show's creators

Normand Latourelle
Production Design and Art Direction

Normand Latourelle did not grow up on a farm. He has never felt closer to horses than to humans. He had never even ridden a horse until just recently. What first sparked his imagination was a performance of the *Les Légendes Fantastiques* show in Drummondville, which he designed. For this multimedia fresco, he had developed a scene presenting the birth of a village, with a hundred or so performers... and one horse. Despite the large number of incredibly talented performers and the captivating special effects, the animal always stole the show. "It was definitely a born performer!" Normand says with a laugh. When some envious individuals suggested dropping the horse from the show, Normand decided to add more instead. Upon witnessing the audience's positive response, he decided that, one day, he would put on a show starring these fascinating creatures.

Cavalia's philosophy

Normand Latourelle soon began learning all he could about horses and developing a philosophy based on respecting their right to freedom. He says, "During my research, I learned how these noble animals lived in the wild. My intent was to reproduce their original environment on stage. My primary concern was how to use horses in a show without exploiting them. I strongly believe that this is not an animal that should be dominated, but rather, a partner and a fellow performer, each one with its own unique personality. That's why I make the stage a huge playground for the horses. When you see them joyfully playing with the performers and trainers, it dawns on you that this is the key to success. Cavalia's philosophy involves creating a healthy environment for the horses before, during and after the show. We are very sensitive to their needs, habits and emotions. Since we consider them a part of our big family, we do everything we can to ensure their well-being. I'm very proud of what we've accomplished."

After starting up the *Cavalia* show, Normand Latourelle wanted to go a step further. When doing the preparation work leading up to *Odysseo*, the first people he met with at the training centre in Sutton were the main horse trainers. He watched the performers and horses having fun as they worked, developing close bonds and spending hours upon hours together, learning gradually. Normand knew that his expectations had been met when he saw that a large number of performers were constantly interrelating during *Odysseo*'s preparation. He was thrilled to see how joyfully everyone worked. His team's pleasant state of mind gave Normand Latourelle a new idea: to conceive an equestrian show that defied the limits of what was possible. He says: "Witnessing the horses running freely and seeing the genuine bonds between the animals and performers, that's what the public loved the most about the first show. The same magical atmosphere is established in *Odysseo*, but here, I wanted to push the bounds of what had been achieved so far with horses. In one entrancing scene, 42 horses with no bridles run freely, only steps away from the audience. What a gorgeous portrayal of freedom! I also think it's perfectly natural when one horse breaks away from the herd to play by itself for a while. In fact, when the horses don't follow the script, it results in some visually delightful moments. My wish, first and foremost, is to have all our horses freely express their true nature. The more freedom we give these animals, the more they open up to us."

The success of a production as grandiose as *Odysseo* is made possible by the solid friendships developed between all members of the team. Normand considers himself very fortunate that all the designers, and everyone associated with the *Odysseo* project, have agreed to lend an unconditional hand in this huge, bold undertaking. Normand's immense pride in his team is apparent when he says, "Even if this mad project only took shape as it was developing, even if there wasn't a well-defined plan from the start, I always considered it crucial to give everyone involved plenty of room and freedom. I never reject an idea before carefully examining it, whether it comes from a groom, an administrator, an executive producer, a director, a designer or any other collaborator or employee. My role in this team is to spark creativity and to listen, observe, direct. In short, my job is to understand and consider the ideas presented to me."

Since the performance space was of utmost importance to him, Normand Latourelle drew sketches with set designer Guillaume Lord. He then met with stage director Wayne Fowkes; costume designers Michèle Hamel and Georges Lévesque; Olivier Goulet from Geodezik, for the 3D images; composer Michel Cusson, for the music; and myself, for the lyrics. However, according to Normand, *Odysseo* holds up in large part due to the tireless work put in by technical director James Richardson, who acted as a go-between for the creators and the workshop, construction and assembly teams. The show's success is also largely due to the continued dedication of Normand's son Mathieu, whom he had just named executive producer and who helped bring *Odysseo* to life.

In his 40-year career in the performing arts, Normand Latourelle had a chance to explore several disciplines: lighting, sound, record production, music publishing, talent management, production management, directing, artistic management and artistic direction. Born in Montréal, Quebec, Canada, he was only 13 when he organized his first show. He became a self-taught talent agent at the age of 16. After participating in Cirque du Soleil's development from 1985 to 1990, he went on to create several large-scale events. Far-seeing and eager to try his hand at everything, Normand Latourelle likes to surprise audiences with things they've never seen before. He keeps finding new ways to combine different forms of artistic expression and reinvent the performance space. Since 2003, he has been completely invested in Cavalia, pouring all of his talent, imagination and passion into his company.

Unveiled in 2003, the *Cavalia* show continues to wow audiences around the globe. After a resoundingly successful tour throughout Canada, the United States and Mexico, it received standing ovations in Belgium, Spain, Portugal, Germany and the Netherlands, as well as in Australia, Singapore, Taiwan, South Korea, Hong Kong and the United Arab Emirates. It is now well-established in China. Since 2011, *Odysseo*, following in *Cavalia*'s footsteps, has dazzled over a million spectators in Mexico and Canada (Toronto, Calgary, Winnipeg, Edmonton, Vancouver, Montréal, Québec City and Laval). The company is currently touring major cities in the United States: Los Angeles (where it was invited on the *Tonight Show*), Atlanta, Denver, Dallas, Seattle, Boston, Washington, San Francisco, Burbank, Irvine, Scottsdale, Salt Lake City and Miami. It goes without saying that *Cavalia* and *Odysseo*'s reputation around the globe is helping spread word of the made-in-Quebec creative genius. In fact, Normand Latourelle was decorated by the Ordre national du Québec in 2007, in recognition of the excellence of his body of work.

Wayne Fowkes
Directing

A director's job is to harmonize a wide variety of artistic and technical events. Coordinating a large number of performers and technicians requires both logic and intuition. One of Wayne Fowkes' greatest qualities is his ability to unify the 15 or so scenes in *Odysseo* and make them flow. This show stays the course because the director not only gives every scene its own rhythm, but also ensures a smooth transition from one to the next.

"Whether a play, music show, ballet or opera, the important thing is pacing, to keep the audience captivated. If the rhythm is too slow, people get bored. If it's too quick, the audience doesn't have time to appreciate it. Giving spectators the impression that time is standing still, that an hour has sped by in 20 minutes... that's what I do," he says.

A former singer, dancer and actor, Wayne Fowkes' knowledge of music, of movement onstage, of a show's theatrical dimension and of technology gives him both the ability to sum up what is important and to pay attention to the smallest detail. *Odysseo*'s ability to enchant audiences through multiple media is in large part thanks to Wayne's artistic talent. A flexible, meticulous leader, he found a way to unify the show's dynamic and meditative content.

Originally from Leeds, Great Britain, Wayne Fowkes now lives in Austria with his family. Wayne started out as a singer and dancer in London's West End, performing in several large shows. His career path led him to explore choreography and artistic direction for television productions in Great Britain and the rest of Europe, among others. By the age of 30, he was working as Andrew Lloyd Webber's artistic director. In 2000, he started at the Millenium Dome, an immense London show hall, as artistic coordinator. That same year, he became artistic director of the much-celebrated *Notre-Dame de Paris* musical (and its subsequent adaptation into eight languages) and, in 2004, of the *Don Juan* musical. In 2007, he made his directing debut with the *Butterflies* musical, performed in Beijing. Although this is his first time working with horses and while the equestrian world in *Odysseo* is quite different from the musicals he is used to, this unique adventure has revealed new dimensions to his talent.

Michel Cusson
Original Music

Michel Cusson's music forms the heart of *Odysseo*. The variety of his rhythms and subtlety of his melodies fill spectators with emotion. For the composer, *Odysseo* is a reminder of the basic human need to have a connection with nature. The horses were his muse and the music he composed gives them a voice.

Normand Latourelle asked to meet with Michel Cusson one day, to discuss a large-scale show under the largest big top in the world, with more horses and performers gracing the stage than in *Cavalia*, for which Michel had composed the score. An inexperienced composer might have leaned toward something huge and Hollywoodesque, with crashing drums and trumpets, but Michel Cusson is convinced that audiences prefer to be gently rocked into dreamland. Like a master of the martial arts, he has great power and strength, but rarely needs to use them. This way, he saves his energy and does more, and better, with less. "Since the horse is a very refined animal,

I wanted to create supple, elegant music that leaves more room for flexibility, quicker movements and more subtlety in translating the emotion in a given moment."

The composer knew that the concept of the show was a journey through some of the most gorgeous landscapes on the planet. He therefore suggested that he and production designer and artistic director Normand Latourelle listen to a selection of ethnic-flavoured world music. In search of which instruments would best suit the *Odysseo* show, Normand and Michel agreed that the music should not be electric, but rather acoustic, organic. After seeing the immensity of the big top and the three-dimensional images, the composer took the risk of creating completely unpretentious music, music that is more intimate, more minimalistic, warmer, more humble... Music that is capable of capturing the most subtle of emotions.

The composer and musicians continuously refine the score. Like in jazz, even if the music is set down on paper, the musicians, all of high caliber, are able to improvise and adapt to what is taking place onstage.

Michel Cusson's work, both in the legendary jazz-rock fusion group UZEB and on the big and small screens (25 movies and 19 television series) has earned him a number of prestigious awards in Quebec and Canada, including 14 Félix awards, 6 Gémeaux, 7 SOCAN, 1 Jutra and 1 Gemini. His musical contribution also extends to creating original scores for large-scale shows like *Cavalia*. *Odysseo* marked the fourth time he and Normand Latourelle worked together. Once more, Michel Cusson was able to create, for the horses, performers and spectators, music that evokes a wide range of emotion.

Raôul Duguay
Poetic Texts and Song Lyrics

Poet, philosopher, painter, sculptor, composer and singer, Raôul Duguay is a prolific creator and versatile communicator. In his 50-year career, this wakeful dreamer has published 16 books of poetry, recorded 16 albums and given over 3 000 shows. He has received several awards in recognition of his poetic works, including the Félix-Antoine Savard award presented during the International Poetry Festival, the *Mérite du français dans la culture* award presented by the *Office québécois de la langue française* and the *Prix à la création artistique en région* presented by the *Conseil des arts et des lettres du Québec*. He first began collaborating with Normand Latourelle in the early 1980s. Raôul co-wrote the lyrics and songs for *Légendes fantastiques*, a large-scale show by Normand Latourelle that won gold during the *Gala des Grands Prix du tourisme québécois* in 1998-1999. Finally, his famous song *"La Bittt à Tibi"* was inducted in the Canadian Songwriters Hall of Fame in 2008. An idea-person, documentalist and poet, Raôul Duguay has worked with Cavalia since the adventure began in 2003, writing several poetic texts and the lyrics to the songs used in *Odysseo*.

Guillaume Lord
Set Design

A set designer's main role is to draw the performance space and, in *Odysseo's* case, translate Normand Latourelle's vision of horses roaming free in the wild. Guillaume Lord came in long before the costumes, lighting and projections and, like an architect, determined where the horses and performers would enter and exit the stage, the position of the big screen, the strip decorating the forestage, the angle of the stands, the position of the water intake for the lake, the slope of the mountain, the trees "growing" on the sides, the positioning of the musicians, etc. In fact, with the exception of the exterior of the big top, he is the one who designed all of the scenery before the plans were submitted to the engineers and builders. Of course, Guillaume Lord had to carefully plan the ideal curve for the path the horses would follow onstage, to ensure that they could move around and gallop in complete comfort and safety.

In fact, a set designer translates dream into reality, poetry into engineering.

In Canada and abroad, Guillaume Lord is known as a versatile set designer with a very fertile creative imagination. He lends his talent to the theatre, circus arts, dance, variety shows, rock concerts and musicals. With Cavalia's latest creation, he had to design a set that would suit both the four-legged and two-legged performers.

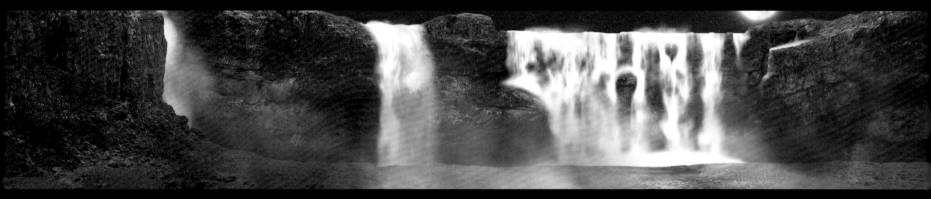

Geodezik
Visual Design

Geodezik is a Quebec-based multimedia design firm specialized in video production and the design of broadcasting systems for shows, public events and permanent art installations. The company also offers set design and architectural design consulting services and takes a global view of multimedia, from a project's initial design to its very last performance. Geodezik creates original content and new technologies with the help of a community of visual-arts and new-media artists. *Odysseo*'s visual environment is discrete and features an ideal blend of lighting and scenery, which perfectly suited Geodezik's artistic approach.

There is no doubt that *Odysseo*'s success is in large part due to the creative imagination of the Geodezik team, whose images were inspired by wild horse habitats around the world and the beauty of nature in these protected environments. After helping to develop and integrate projection in the

scenery, Geodezik designed and added the images to the show's set design. Since *Odysseo*'s big top, and therefore the stage, are of a size never before seen, the team had to find a scale for the projected images that would make them as realistic as possible. Thanks to the 3D images created by Geodezik, the audience is taken on a voyage to places that may appear familiar, but do not exist in the real world. The illusion of vastness is mainly due to the realism of the images and the deft use of perspectives that support this visual effect.

Alain Lortie
Lighting Design

A stage as vast as *Odysseo*'s requires innovative lighting. Alain Lortie, master lighting technician, had a sizeable challenge on his hands. He could not light the projection screen, since that would affect the quality of the three-dimensional landscape images prepared by the Geodezik team. In a standard show, the lighting technician will use smoke or fog to give the light beams volume, dimension and presence. In this way, the lighting technician is like a painter. His canvas is black and the light beams projected onto the smoke are the equivalent of brush strokes. But since it would have been difficult for the horses to see where they were going, Alain Lortie had to forego the smoke and fog and instead target the forest-curtain, the large tulle screen, the slope of the mountain and the ground. Instead of painting in space, he bathed these set design elements with light to give them texture. This way, he was able to give the impression that the video images projected on the giant screens and the ground lighting are in perfect and magical continuity.

Even though the set is exceptionally large, the spectators must always have a full view of what is taking place onstage. Like on a film set, the lighting technician highlights certain set design elements by playing around with zoom, close-ups, fields of view and reverse angle shots. Sometimes he also isolates a visual element by shining a spotlight on it.

Thanks to advances in lighting technology, some incredible effects are now possible. Alain Lortie explains: "Today, lighting designers use little robots, or smart lights. In *Odysseo*, each of the 100 projectors I use have 30 or so controls or parameters. This gives me a great deal of control over my programming. Each projector can light up the location I want, at the colour intensity and light beam length I want. The effects are programmed in the console, a computer that saves all the images I've created. The symbiosis between the set designer, video projectionist, musicians and stage director is vital when comes time for the final light mixing."

In a show featuring horses and acrobats, the lighting technician must ensure that, in the midst of the action, everyone can see where they are going and not be blinded by the lights. To get the horses used to the lighting, which changes frequently, the animals were allowed to roam around onstage from the very first days of rehearsal. Today, when a projector turns on, changes intensity or turns off, the horses do not react.

In fact, the lighting is greatly modified based on the horses' movements. In a living performance like *Odysseo*, the creators and their collaborators must always be prepared to adjust to new practical realities, in order to create a dream world in which the horses feel at home.

Alain Lortie has practiced his profession with great passion for over 30 years, earning himself an excellent reputation in Quebec, France and Asia. Named "lighting designer of the year" a number of times by the *Association québécoise de l'industrie du disque, du spectacle et de la vidéo* (ADISQ), he also received the *Masque des éclairages* and a Dora Mavor Moore award from the Toronto Alliance for the Performing Arts.

Darren Charles
Choreography

Drawing from his vast ballet and contemporary dance experience, as well as from movements both ethnic and acrobatic, Darren Charles incorporates a blend of styles in his choreographies, making them uniquely his own. He lent his eyes and ears to the African acrobats, whose culture is rich in sound colours, rhythms and body movements. By choosing to respect everything natural and spontaneous in these exuberant acrobats and musicians, he was able to shape their artistic and athletic skills into a relevant whole. The choreographies he created with these acrobats and dancers are very lively, radiating humour and joy.

Alain Gauthier
Choreography for The Angels scene

Acrobat and choreographer Alain Gauthier, who worked on Cavalia's first show as well as several other large-scale productions, was once again able to apply his stunt and aerial acrobatics experience. He is the one who choreographed the exquisite "The Angels" scene.

Elsie Morin and Mathieu Roy "Les Oiseaux du Paradis"

Choreography for Carosello *scene and design of the rotating poles*

A trained dancer, Elsie Morin has 25 years of experience in the arts as a choreographer and performer. Highly imaginative, she favours light, flowing movements that perfectly capture *Odysseo*'s essence and mood.

Mathieu Roy has worked in show business since 1990, first as an artist, then as dance instructor and designer. His most recent works are filled with grace, strength and elegance, creating unforgettably captivating moments.

The acrobatic designers and choreographers of *Odysseo*'s magical "*Carosello*" scene, Elsie and Mathieu have worked as a team for several years under the name *Les Oiseaux du Paradis* and participated in shows in 20 or so countries.

Georges Lévesque (1951-2011)
and Michèle Hamel
Costumes Design

Georges Lévesque and Michèle Hamel, *Odysseo*'s costume designers, worked together for 35 years. It is rare to see such complicity between two creators, one from the fashion world and the other from the world of theatre and film. "We were a great team," says Michèle Hamel. "One would start the sketch for a costume and the other would finish it. Four hands on the same drawing, that's rare and wonderful."

Sadly, Georges Lévesque passed away on the eve of *Odysseo*'s opening. The entire team was deeply saddened by the loss of this invaluable artist; Michèle, most of all.

Georges Lévesque and Michèle Hamel came up with the idea for the show's costumes during a conversation with Normand Latourelle and Wayne Fowkes. Normand wanted to evoke tribes, nomadic and sedentary people as well as wild and imaginary lands. After perusing historical illustrations, the duo sketched and made prototypes, tried them on the performers and quickly realized that balancing creativity and practicality, looks and safety, while also giving the costumes an exotic flair would be no easy task. However, they pulled it off with great success, making costumes adapted to the mood in each scene of *Odysseo*.

Choosing the right fabric was another challenge. The most practical solution would have been to make the costumes out of stretchy material, but perhaps to compete with the beauty of the horses' coats, the designers wanted beautiful fabrics, natural textiles, silk, chiffon, noble materials that would highlight the fluidity of the movements, catch the light and draw attention to the elegance of the performers' figures. However, Georges and Michèle had to make concessions in the cut so that the costumes would be practical for the performers and horses, who are in constant motion during the show.

Each costume was made in 15 samples. At the height of production, three costume workshops were running full time.

A true non-conforming artist, Montréal designer Georges Lévesque started his career in the early 1970s, pursuing a dream of beauty without compromise. In addition to creating clothing lines, he designed the stage costumes of several well-known performers. He was the costumer for over 30 shows in different artistic disciplines, a world he felt at home in, having started out as an actor and dancer.

Michèle Hamel, also from Montréal, started working as a costume designer in 1977, when she met director Gilles Carle. Her name appears in the credits of some 50 Canadian film and television productions and she has received numerous awards (Gémeaux, Jutra, Génie) for her work.

It is thanks to their respective talents, unique style and vast experience that these two designers were able to cement their enviable reputation.

Jessica Manzo
Makeup

The stage under *Odysseo*'s big top is the largest ever built. From a distance, humans appear smaller and therefore need to be more expressive to be better seen. The same is true for makeup. The facial features must be made bigger, as if magnified, so that from far away, the humans—or the ground, on horseback or on stilts—are more visible and the audience can better read their expressions. Also, depending on the lighting used in each scene, the choice of colours makes the riders' and perfomers' features stand out more.

The greatest advantage to using the appropriate stage makeup is to highlight the perfomers' presence and charisma. "In *Odysseo*, the humans who go out to meet the horse had to be beautiful and noble," explains Jessica.

The makeup is applied in such a way that the people sitting at the very back can see where the eye and cheekbone are located. The goal is to make the faces larger and have the riders and performers look magnificent.

Throughout the show, the riders are seen head-on or from the side. Jessica Manzo takes advantage of this profile line to make the eyebrows stand out. In the facial architecture, the eyebrows indicate where the eye is located and mark the emotion being expressed. Jessica also carefully applies makeup to the neck, creating two shadows on either side of the trachea and adding a light, finely speckled colour. This gives the riders, aerial acrobats and stilt walkers a longer neck. Proud and noble like the horse, shoulders back, all of these beautiful people perform their acts with their heads held very high.

Since the performers do their own makeup before every show, taking this moment to concentrate and slip into their character, Jessica Manzo prepared a booklet for each person, indicating, step by step, how to use her brushes and products. To remember her exact formula, each performer has a picture of their made-up face, accompanied by written instructions.

Inspired by images of the Middle East, the makeup artist created almond-shaped eyes and gorgeous profiles. For the ground performers and riders, she uses warm colours: shades of orange, ochre, bronze and rose. For the aerial artists, she uses cold colours: golden yellow, bright white, crystalline dotted with clear speckles, lime green, cyan clue and black. Since the Guinean artists have dark skin, to make their bone structure stand out, she creates points of light by using bronzes, ochres and golds.

"My goal is to give everyone a joyous appearance, along with stature and strength. Because to my eye, the performers are all kings and queens of different tribes."

Louis Bond
Hair

Hair designer Louis Bond was inspired by the horses' manes. Given that in *Odysseo*, no one would have time to change their hairstyle between scenes, he kept the same look, the same line, especially for the men. However, all of the women are wearing hairpieces. These are braided into their own hair to ensure that their hairstyle does not budge during the acts, no matter how acrobatic. And since there is enough colour on their faces, the costumes and the big screen, Louis Bond decided to let the performers keep their natural hair colour.

151

Big Top on the Wing

Some say it is a strange cathedral
sailing through the clouds, escorted by angels
Some say it is a castle, snow-laden
soaring above a dreamlike kingdom

A miniature village flying from land to land
Odysseo's big top is an island
its treasure, the horse
of beauty and majestic gait

Acrobats, dancers, musicians and riders
sail aboard this enchanted schooner

Great white big top

A true marvel of modern architecture, an immense white big top is home to the *Odysseo* show. Rising majestically from the cityscape, its bright whiteness, immense structure and clean lines are admired by all, who wonder what could be hidden beneath. A mystery!

The doors to dreamland open when the spectators enter the world's largest big top, larger than a football field. A staggering 38 metres (124 feet) high, it boasts a surface area of 7,811 square metres (84,076 square feet) (or 9 912 square metres (106,700 square feet) with the pegs). *Odysseo*'s creators did

not start off with a scenario, but rather an idea: creating a show to celebrate the journey taken by humans and horses. To give the horses as much freedom as they could, they wanted to create the largest possible space. This is why Normand Latourelle drew up the plans for the performance space before finding the big top that would house it. This explains the perfect integration between action and location.

For the first time in the history of big tops, innovative architects and engineers invented a structure worthy of monumental cathedral arches.

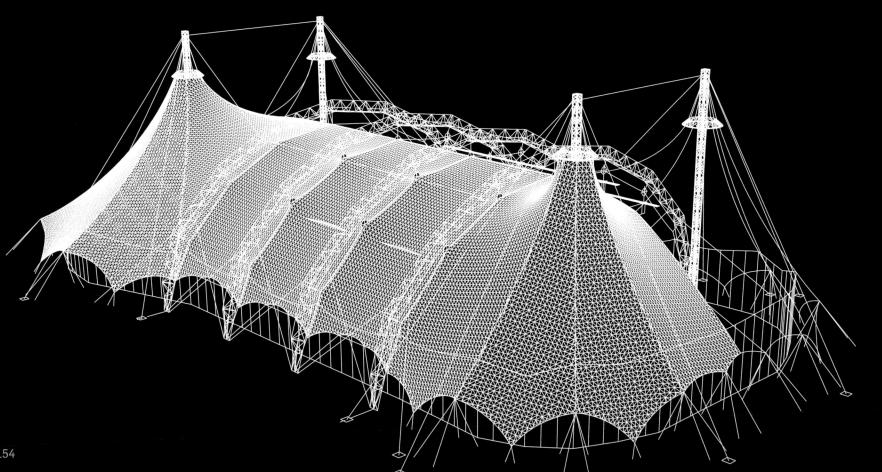

The *Odysseo* big top is 73 metres (351 feet) long and 73 metres (240 feet) wide. The stands seat 2 000 facing a stage that measures 1,626 square metres (17,500 square feet) by itself. The seating curves slightly around the stage, so the audience can experience the horses up close. In building the stage, teams transported 15,000 metric tons (16,535 tons) of material, a special blend of sand, soil and stone, to form the 13-metre-high (43-foot-high) mountain.

The tent poles are an impressive 38 metres (124 feet) high and no support structures or metal posts block the view of the stage. Inside the big top, the technical grid, installed 27 metres (89 feet) off the ground, holds 80 metric

tons (88 tons) of material: set components and pieces of equipment that are lifted and lowered as needed during the show. A total of 173 different types of motors run all of the suspended equipment, likely a record for a touring show of this type. Three arches, absolute marvels of engineering, support the big top. It takes a 250-metric-ton (276-ton) crane to install all of the material. In short, the 1,626 square metres (17,500 square feet) stage forms the world's largest performance space under a big top. From a strictly technical standpoint, creating this gigantic structure meant truly pushing the bounds of technology. Nothing of its kind has ever been designed and built. It is under this impressive structure that a moving tribute is paid to the nobility of nature and the horse.

Mathieu Latourelle, Executive Producer, and a significant contributor to the project, says: "Other companies have done extraordinary things, but we pushed the limits of technology and set design. I believe that we truly revolutionized big top shows."

Says Normand Latourelle: "*Odysseo* is the incredible journey taken by exceptional teams. The individuals on this voyage share an ambition: to be the best in the world. So much effort and so many hours have been poured into this project... Of course, the show is at the heart of our business, but the individuals and teams that support it are just as important. Together, they make this odyssey a guaranteed success!"

Village on tour

Odysseo is a nomadic show, travelling from city to city in North America and soon around the world.

This magical, all-white village made up of the big top and its adjacent facilities disappears from a city's skyline one day to appear in another the next, like a spacecraft arriving from a mysterious planet...

A huge family of nearly 200 people and 67 horses of 11 different breeds make up this village's population, blending numerous nationalities, languages and cultures. To feel at home on tour, everyone must keep an open mind while continually adapting to different customs, environments and climates.

Brennan Figari, the aerial acrobat who balances in his hoop high up in the air, is from San Francisco. He would have loved for the show to always stay in his city, because he misses his family and the birthdays and weddings he is unable to attend. On the other hand, he enjoys travelling: "We're all learning. When you're on tour, you're a family. No family is perfect. You don't always get along with everyone. There are so many different cultures and languages, so many differences between us. But learning together brings us closer. Although we don't necessarily understand the way everyone thinks, we can respect it. When we're onstage together, what we feel is joy."

Kevin Ouellet, Chief Electrician, tells me that in addition to being a huge show, Odysseo has made his dreams come true: heading off on an adventure, travelling, meeting people, seeing new things, enjoying a change of scenery.

Like most people who travel for work, Guylaine Dempsey, Director of Public Services, misses her house. "I do well on tour because I like to travel and meet people, but I still feel far from home. Every month, my husband comes to visit me. When we see each other, we make time for what is important and enjoy little treats, like making apple crisp together. That makes us happy."

Although Annick Gouaillier, Odysseo's stage manager, has worked in many theatres, she finds that working under a huge big top is quite different and challenging. "What motivates me," she says, "is that I can practice my profession on a daily basis and, despite all the difficulties that arise on tour, I enjoy travelling and exploring new cultures. However, I really am quite a homebody. I like to putter around the house. What is fascinating is that every two months, I get to discover a new place to buy bread. It's fun to discover local products, local wines."

Marc-Olivier Leprohon, Director of Artistic and Equestrian Operations, has been on tour for six years. His job is to follow up with the team, which means that he is in contact with everyone. If necessary, he flies the creators out to the new city, arranging their transportation and lodging. "We're a family. The performers love what they do. You can feel their passion when they're onstage. No one views what they're doing as a job. What we emanate during a performance is who we are offstage. We love interacting with the public and the public is happy to share beautiful moments of creativity and joy with us."

Nicolas Vandenplas, Stable Manager, has spent a good part of his life–about 20 years–around horses. He is unmarried, with no children, by choice. He has tried being sedentary, but it just does not seem to suit him at the moment. He enjoys frequently changing cities, taking on new challenges, building and breaking down the set, rebuilding everything, hiring local people as grooms every six to eight weeks, etc. During that time, the horses are on vacation in nature and he is delighted for them.

The most difficult aspect of touring is coordinating everyone according to the set plan. To reach the final goal, many different people need to work together. People in charge of logistics cannot be unaware of what the technicians are doing. Logistics and human resources management are crucial to making sure that each person's efforts are serving the same goal, while respecting the deadlines. All of the company's departments are interdependent.

Odysseo,
cultural crossroads

Performers and professionals of a dozen nationalities, speaking no less than seven different languages, work together on a daily basis. Among the Guinean artists, some belong to tribes. They share the same living and working spaces as Muslim Russians, Catholic Russians, Christian Americans, as well as Quebecers and Europeans, believers and non-believers alike. Despite this incredible cultural diversity, and because no animosity is tolerated within the team – a true league of nations – everyone gets along and respects one another. And, due to their incredible sensitivity, the horses, without being aware of it, keep the peace between the men and women who walk among them.

Right from the start, Odysseo's team have to follow a few ground rules : the acrobats have to learn how to ride and the riders have to learn acrobatics. Since each learns the other's discipline, everyone is able to speak the other's language, to communicate and to understand one another. When all of the performers meet to break bread at the same table, they develop beautiful friendships while sharing their points of view. By keeping an open mind, everyone learns sharing and tolerance on a daily basis. This is a very effective means of transcending religious, linguistic and political differences and thus of preserving the harmony vital to the success of a huge undertaking like *Odysseo*.

Interdependence

For Normand Latourelle and his team, what matters most in interpersonal relationships is creating situations and a psychological environment conducive to interdependence and cooperation. It is because they enjoy working together that all members of the *Odysseo* team exude passion for what they do. The equestrian director even came up with a welcome ritual. When new performers are hired, they are asked to dance and express themselves spontaneously before their fellow performers, who stand in a circle, clapping enthusiastically to welcome the new person to the team. This humanistic relationship between performers is also experienced with the horses. The happy energy that emanates when the humans and horses play together lets each rediscover their inner child.

For the show to run smoothly, every person and department concerned must be interdependent. According to James Richardson, Technical Director: "What touches me most about *Odysseo* is the artistic team. Most of the members are very young, almost all in their 20s. And they tackle things with incredible speed. But what astonishes and pleases me is to see them integrate patience during the learning process. It's wonderful to see them at work. The exemplary valour these young people display is eye-opening."

The Joy of Being Together

Odysseo is the largest and most complex touring show in the world. The talent, dedication and energy the performers invest is impressive. And few have show-business training. Some attended riding schools or, like the Guineans, entertained passers-by on a beach. According to Mathieu Latourelle, Executive Producer: "This gathering of artists from different backgrounds is a marvellous combination in a show of international scope. When I watch them perform, I'm pleased to see that they're having fun. Their joy in being together has a huge effect on the audience."

Passion

A rare phenomenon in a large team like *Odysseo*'s, hierarchy is not what dictates behaviours and relationships. Ramon Molina-Gonzalez, rider and Equestrian Director on Tour, thinks that this is the way to go: "Everyone is equal. There are no superstars. Everyone knows their strengths and the others' strengths. It's a passion for the show and the horses that leads everyone to combine their skills. And every individual is important, because the team energy always needs to be up. If a performer or a horse is absent, it's not the end of the world. Either the person or animal is replaced or another solution is found so that the show can go on."

The people who work on the *Odysseo* show are a passionate bunch. If you ask them what they do for a living, they will tell you about the human richness they experience as members of this community.

Breeds and names of the *Odysseo* horses

Our Four-Legged Performers

Odysseo's stables house 67 horses of 11 different breeds, originating from seven countries throughout North America and Europe: Spain, Portugal, France, the Netherlands, Germany, the United States and Canada. These magnificent steeds are all males, either stallions or geldings. Their average age is 10. The youngest recruit is 5 years old and the eldest horse is 15.

Since the millennium-old relationship between humans and horses forms the heart of Cavalia's shows, the company fosters a working environment where patience, trust and deep respect for the animals reign. The training methods are based on the belief that the horses should have fun while learning and performing. The trainers are therefore very careful to tailor their requests to the performance level the horses are ready to offer.

The Names of Our Horses

Acero (Spanish Purebred)
Andaluz (Lusitano)
Atila (Spanish Purebred)
Aureolo (Spanish Purebred)
Bacilon (Spanish Purebred)
Bello (Spanish Purebred)
Borracho (Spanish Purebred)
Bravas (Arabian)
Bud (Quarter Horse)
California (Quarter Horse)
Carlo (Lusitano)
Chief (Arabian)
Choice (Arabian)
Disparate (Lusitano)
Django (Quarter Horse)
Djigtit (Quarter Horse)
Eagle (Quarter Horse)
Frosty (Arabian)
Garuda (Paint Horse)
Geegee (Arabian)
Greco (Spanish Purebred)
Gus (Arabian)
Hawk (Quarter Horse)
Indigo (Appaloosa)
Jazzy (Canadian)
Kofre (Lusitano)
Lazao (Lusitano)
Lover (Arabian)
Max (Paint Horse)
Milor (Quarter Horse)
Motion (Arabian)
Nezma (Arabian)
Nugget (half-Arabian)
Numerario (Spanish Purebred)

Octanium (Arabian)
Omerio (Lusitano)
Opinel (Lusitano)
Osioso (Lusitano)
Pat (Quarter Horse)
Patof (Warmblood)
Pearl (Arabian)
Petrolo (Lusitano)
Ponpon (Canadian)
Quetzal (Holsteiner)
Quiebro (Spanish Purebred)
Ripple (Quarter Horse)
Romeo (Quarter Horse)
Roucio (Quarter Horse)
Samba (Lusitano)
Sandrino (Lusitano)
Shake (Arabian)
Sherry (Spanish Purebred)
Silver (Arabian)
Tango (Quarter Horse)
Timeo (Appaloosa)
Tiopepe (Spanish Purebred)
Traje (Lusitano)
Trepador (Lusitano)
Trujal (Spanish Purebred)
Tunante (Spanish Purebred)
Tunique (Oldenburg)
Univoco (Lusitano)
Vareto (Lipizzaner)
Xadrez (Lusitano)
Xuto (Lusitano)
Zain (Arabian)
Zinco (Lusitano)

Odysseo Horse Breeds

APPALOOSA – First bred in the 18th century by the Nez Percés Native American tribe in Idaho (United States), the Appaloosa became the state's official horse in 1975. It can be identified by its striped hooves and colourfully speckled coat. Formerly called the "Palouse horse," it was named after the Palouse River, which flows through the breed's native states of Washington and Idaho.

ARABIAN – Known for its distinctive concave profile, large eyes and lively intelligence, the Arabian horse has lived among the desert tribes of the Arabian Peninsula for thousands of years. Raised by the Bedouins as war horses capable of withstanding extreme weather conditions, this breed developed unmatched drive and endurance. Its bond with humans is well known: Arabian horses often shared a tent, food and water with their nomadic riders.

CANADIAN – A sadly undiscovered gem, the Canadian is a descendent of the horses sent to the New World by King Louis XIV of France. Nicknamed "little iron horse," it is known for its strength, eagerness, curiosity and resistance to harsh climates. This courageous equine has been endangered in the past, but its population has now risen to 2 500 individuals.

HOLSTEINER – Presumably the oldest of the Warmblood breeds, the Holsteiner made its appearance in northern Germany in the 13th century. While there are relatively few of these horses, they dominate international show jumping competitions, in addition to making their mark in dressage, carriage driving, hound hunting and three-day events. They can be identified by their arched and rather high neck, as well as their powerful hindquarters.

LIPIZZANER – The Lipizzaner was named after the city of Lipica, in Slovenia (Southern Europe). Bred in the 16th century for the imperial court of Austria, this breed, symbolic of the Spanish Riding School of Vienna, excels in the art of classical dressage. During the Second World War, bombings and famine threatened the breed's survival. Luckily, stallions were evacuated to St. Martin, Austria, where U.S. General George S. Patton and his army were based. A lover of horses, General Patton, in collaboration with Colonel Alois Podhajsky, director of the Spanish Riding School, ensured the breed's protection. Their actions helped save 250 Lipizzaners, thus preserving the breed.

LUSITANO – Bold and athletic, the Lusitano is the breed traditionally used by Portuguese bullfighters and is venerated by Portugal's classical riding masters. Its build is similar to the Spanish Purebred. Legend has it that the two breeds have the same lineage, originating from the Iberian Peninsula a few thousand years ago. In 1960, Portugal closed its genealogical books to Spanish horses, changing the breed's name to "Lusitano." Identified by its abundant mane and tail, the Lusitano has a convex profile, with the bridge of its nose reminiscent of ancient Andalusian or Iberian horses.

OLDENBURG – The Oldenburg was developed by crossing ancient Friesian breeds, originating from the borderland between the Netherlands and Germany. Admired for its elegance and flowing movements, the Oldenburg grew in popularity after the Second World War.

PAINT HORSE – Known for the colorful patterns on its piebald or skewbald coat, as well as its compact build and docile nature, the paint horse is very popular around the world. Its coat can combine white with all the other colours on the equine spectrum. This extremely versatile breed is the second most popular in the United States.

SPANISH PUREBRED (P.R.E.) – This breed's history is closely intertwined with Andalusian culture. A horse with a luxurious mane, incredible charisma and great beauty, its origins date back nearly 4 000 years. Thanks to its agility and lithe movements, the Spanish Purebred grew in popularity in the courts of Europe and in equestrian academies on the Old Continent from the 15th to the 18th centuries. In 1912, the Spanish closed their genealogical books to Portugal, renaming the breed *Pura Raza Española* (or P.R.E.) rather than "Andalusian."

QUARTER HORSE – A true speed demon, the Quarter Horse can reach speeds nearing 90 km/hr (55 mph) in races of 400 metres (1312 feet) or less (quarter mile); hence, its name, which stems from its ability to beat other breeds in these races. Known for its versatility, even temperament and "cow sense," the Quarter Horse is the world's most popular horse, with over 4 million individuals registered. Compact, muscular and intelligent, the Quarter Horse is the icon of Western-style riding.

WARMBLOOD – Frequent winner of international circuits, the Warmblood excels at show jumping and dressage, making it a breed of choice for Olympic equestrian teams around the world. This breed is the result of crossing sturdy draft horses with hot-blooded Arabians captured in battle in the Middle East and Africa. The breed became more popular after the Second World War, when pleasure riding spread throughout the western world.

The *Odysseo* team

Odysseo creators

NORMAND LATOURELLE
Production Designer and Artistic Director

WAYNE FOWKES
Stage Director

MICHEL CUSSON
Composer

RAÔUL DUGUAY
Lyricist

GUILLAUME LORD
Set Designer

GEODEZIK
Visual Designer

**GEORGES LÉVESQUE
AND MICHÈLE HAMEL**
Costume Designers

ALAIN LORTIE
Lighting Designer

DARREN CHARLES
Choreographer

ALAIN GAUTHIER
Choreographer of the "The Angels" scene

ELSIE MORIN AND MATHIEU ROY
Choreographers for *Carosello* scene and
designers of the rotating poles

LOUIS BOND
Hair Designer

JESSICA MANZO
Makeup Artist

Pre-production

MATHIEU TARDIF-LATOURELLE
Executive Producer

JAMES RICHARDSON
Technical Director

BENOIT FONTAINE
Logistics Director

RACHÈLE BÉLANGER
Director of Artistic Operations

BRUNO RAFIE
Assistant to the Lighting Designer

YAMOUSSA BANGOURA
composer and lyricist of "Dounya"

FABRIZIO VOGHERA
Italian adaptation of Raôul Duguay's poems

PHILIPPE CHARTRAND
Acrobatic Trainer

SAMUEL ALVAREZ
Aerial Trainer

GUENNADI TOUAEV
Cossack Trick-Riding Trainer

LOUIS CÔTÉ
Stage Manager

DARREN CHARLES
Choreographer

RUTH JOYAL
Assistant to the Stage Director

MAGALIE CRINON
Assistant to the Equestrian Director

MARC-OLIVIER LEPROHON
Assistant to the Equestrian Director

MARTIN LYONNAIS
Production Assistant

CRISTEL RICHER
Assistant to the Set Designer

JULIE MEASROCH
Assistant to the Stage Manager

CHANTAL SIMARD
Costume Assistant

VÉRONIQUE GAGNON
Costume Assistant

JENNY LYNN MANZO
Makeup Assistant

SUZANNE TRÉPANIER
Makeup Assistant

MARYSE LEPROHON
Hair Assistant

MANON DESMARAIS
Costume Consultant

NATHALIE DUGAS
Shoe Consultant

ANDRÉ BOULAIS
Manager of the *Odysseo* stables

PIERRE JORDACHE
Head Technical Rigger

SCOTT ENGLAND
Head Rigger

NICOLAS BRODEUR
Rigger

NICOLAS GENDRON
Video Operator

SÉBASTIEN PEDNAULT
Lighting Operator

GUY HÉBERT
Sound Mixer

OLIVIER OUELLETTE
Head Video Technician

MATHIEU BEAULIEU
Chief Electrician

DOMINIC RIVARD-PROULX
Head Sound Engineer

JANELLE LÉVESQUE
Draftsperson

DEBRA LEE LAMOTHE
Project Manager

ÉTIENNE LABRECQUE
Project Manager

AIMÉ VINCENT
Technical Project Manager

OLIVIER FOREST
Head Carpenter

CLAUDE ST-AMANT
Site Manager

GUY ROSSIGNOL
Big Top Consultant

ERIK JAEGER
Big Top Consultant

BRIAN BILODEAU
Kitchen Project Manager

JACKIE DETTWILER
Logistical Project Manager

SIMON TRUDEAU
Logistical Project Manager

NORMAND MALO
Electrician

Board of directors

NORMAND LATOURELLE
Chairperson

DOMINIQUE DAY
Vice-President

PHILIPPE-DENIS RICHARD
Secretary-Treasurer

Administration

NORMAND LATOURELLE
President and Artistic Director

DOMINIQUE DAY
Co-Founder and Executive Vice-President

DAVID TARDIF-LATOURELLE
Vice-President, Market Development and
Legal Affairs

JEAN–BERNARD LAGUE
Vice-President, Finances and Administration
and Chief Financial Officer

DUNCAN FISHER
Vice-President of Operations

VALÉRIE DEJOIE
Corporate Controller

CYNTHIA DUFOUR
Legal Advisor

ANA GRAY RICHARDSON-BACHAND
Legal Advisor

JOCELYN LANGELIER
Tour Logistics Manager

RAYMOND LABRIE
Director of Information Technology

MARTIN LECLERC
Chief Accountant

ARMANDA TEIXEIRA
Payroll Manager

TATIANA LAPOINTE
Payroll Technician

JULIE ROUSSEAU
Recrutment and Human Resources Advisor

SOKUN CHIM
Tour Accountant

ARIYA KONGKHAM
Tour Bookkeeper

MARIE-JOSÉE DASILVA
Accounts Payable Clerk

MARIE-PIER LAVOIE-SIGOUIN
Accounts Receivable Clerk

PETER SOBCZYK
Supervisor, Market Development
and Permits

GUILLAUME PAQUETTE
Coordinator, Market Development
and Permits

DOMINIC RIVARD-PROULX
Transportation Manager

JACKIE DETTWILER
Manager – Site Technician

LORI-ANN YELLE
Operations Coordinator

MARTIN PROULX
Transportation Coordinator

JULIEN PARIS-ROY
Transportation Coordinator

TANYA BESSETTE
Warehouse Manager

Marketing and communications

NANCY MANCINI
Vice-President of Marketing and
Communications

JO-ANNE MARTIN
Director, Development of the Cavalia Brand

ANNIE DUPONT
Director, Media and Sponsorship

MÉLANIE RUEL
Advertising Director

ÉRIC PAQUETTE
Director, Public Relations

SARAH KEMERER
Director, Sales and Promotions

KIM HUARD-CARETTTE
Press Agent

VANESSA FLUSH
Promotion Coordinator

MARIE-CLAUDE BÉRUBÉ
Sales Coordinator

VICTORIA FERNANDEZ
Media Coordinator

JULIE BÉLANGER
Community Manager

ANDRÉS FELIPE LLERENA
Web Developer

ROBERT VIGNOLA
Computer Graphics Technician

JUAN PAULO FLUTSCH PARRA
Web graphic designer

SÈVERINE HORVAT
Coordinator, Development
of the Cavalia Brand

Tour management

NICOLAS ZLICARIC
Tour Manager

Performers

LUCAS ALTEMEWER

SAMUEL ALVAREZ

ALSENY BANGOURA

BALLA MOUSSA BANGOURA

IDRISSA BANGOUROU

ISMAEL BANGOURA

SEKOU CAMARA

ORANE CAUJOLLE-GAZET

MICHEL CHARRON

TOMOKO CHARRON

URIEL CHARTRAND-ARDAIL

ALY CISSE

ISEULYS DESLE

N'FALY DRAME

B.J. ERDMANN

DORIAN ESCALON

STÉPHANIE EVANS

BRENNAN FIGARI

MATHILDE FRAYSSE

LARA GABIN

KAMILA GANCLARSKA

RACHEL GAUTHIER

NEIL GLASER

MARINE GOURDON

ANDREA LEGG

VIRGINIE LOISELLE-BLONDIN

EMMY LOVE

FLORIAN MADRID

YANNIS MADRID

CLÉMENT MESMIN

THÉO MILER

RAMON MOLINA-GONZALEZ

FANNY NEVORET

MAKSYM OVCHYNNIKOV

JULISSA PANUS

ANTOINE ROMANOFF

ALSENY SYLLA

FODE ISMAEL SYLLA

MOHAMED SYLLA

YOUNOUSSA SYLLA

CHELSEA LAYNE TEEL

PAVEL SKYBA

LUCAS TORMIN MENDONÇA

GUENNADI TOUAEV

BATRAZ TSOKOLAEV

ÉLISE VERDONCQ

Musicians

ÉRIC AUCLAIR Bassist, double bassist
and conductor

ÉRIC BOUDREAULT Drummer and
percussionist

SERGE GAMACHE Guitarist

LOUIS-PIER RACICOT Violinist

ANNA-LAURA EDMISTON Singer

Artistic department on tour

MARC-OLIVIER LEPROHON
Director, Artistic and Equestrian Operations

DARREN CHARLES
Resident Artistic Director and Choreographer

MARY-ÈVE MARTEL
Coordinator, Artistic and Equestrian
Operations

RAMON MOLINA GONZALEZ
Resident Equestrian Director

GUENNADI TOUAEV
Cossack Trick-Riding Trainer

ANNICK GOUAILLIER
Stage Manager

ANN-MARIE LÉONARD
Production Assistant

OLIVIER LAPRISE
Production Assistant

JOANNE BAKER
Artistic Therapist

CATHERINE MIREAULT
Head Costumer

CARLEE MILOT
Costumer

KANDY KEIRN SCHWANDT
Costumer

KARINE BRISSON-BOUCHARD
Costumer

Ticket office

CHANTAL ST-CYR
Director, Ticket Office

JORDAN RUIZ
Coordinator, Ticket Office

LAURA PATRICK
Manager, Ticket Office

MAYRA ROBERTSON
Supervisor, Ticket Office

ALEXANDRA BÉDARD-HILLMAN
Supervisor, Ticket Office

ANTOINE LANCTÔT
Supervisor, Call Centre

LOUIS SARMIENTO
Supervisor, Call Centre

ALVARO RODRIGUEZ
Supervisor, Call Centre

NATALIA DE LOS SANTOS
Supervisor, Call Centre

DANIEL BERGERON
Supervisor, Call Centre

KRYSTELLE BISSONNETTE
Supervisor, Call Centre

Technical department

JAMES RICHARDSON
Technical Director

FRÉDÉRICK AUTHIER-PIGEON
Technical Coordinator

JIMMY GARANT
Technical Coordinator

FRANÇOIS GARNEAU
Automation Technician

ALEX BALCER
Rigger

DAVID DOWD
Rigger

FRÉDÉRIC ROUSSEAU
Rigger

PIER-LUC GONZALEZ
Head Carpenter

JEAN-FRANÇOIS TURCOTTE
Carpenter

SARA-ÈVE RIOUX
Carpenter

MARC-ANDRÉ ROY
Carpenter

JONATHAN BICARI
Head Sound Engineer

NICOLAS MICHEL
Monitoring Operator

PASCAL RENAUD
Head of Tour Lighting

MATHIEU BEAULIEU
Assistant to the Head of Tour Lighting

FÉLIX BEZEAU-TREMBLAY
Head of Video and Projections

ÉRIC LANDRY
Lighting and Video Operator

Odysseo stables

NICOLAS VANDENPLAS
Stable Manager

RÉMI GRENIER
Farrier

MARJOLAINE CAMILLE
Veterinary Technician

CAROLANE DUPUIS
Assistant to the Veterinary Technician

RACHÈLE DOSTIE
Equestrian Manager

ADAM STONER
Technician – *Odysseo* stables

PATRICK RATTÉ
Coordinator – *Odysseo* stables

MARIE-CHRISTINE DOSTIE
Groom

VALÉRIE LAUZON
Groom

NEMISKO TESSIER
Groom

JENNIE DESROCHERS
Groom

CLAUDINE LEMIEUX
Groom

JOËLLE RHÉAULT
Groom

NICOLAS LAMOTHE
Groom

CATHERINE ADAMS-GAGNON
Groom

FRANCIS CHAGNON-LAROCQUE
Groom

LUC TESSIER
Groom

ALIX STEGEN
Groom

Logistics

BENOIT FONTAINE
Logistics Director

JOCELYN LÉVESQUE
Site Manager

VERONICA HESS
Logistics Coordinator

KEVEN OUELLET
Head Electrician

VINCENT SÉGUIN–ST-LOUIS
Site Technician

STEVE HALEY
Site Technician

MURRAY WRIGHT
Site Technician

ALEXANDRE MILOT
Site Technician

Public services

GUYLAINE DEMPSEY
Director, Public Services

ALEXIS BÉRIAULT
Food Concessions Supervisor

BRETT COMER
Head Usher

PATRICK NAJOU
Rendez-vous VIP Tent Supervisor

CARMEN MURILLO
Merchandise Supervisor

KHAESARUAI CHOMKHUNTHOT
Merchandise Supervisor

JAKEB FAY DOBSON
Inventory Supervisor

Tour services

JANIE GIROUX
Human Resources and
Tour Services Supervisor

MARIE-CLAUDE DUTIL
Tour Services Coordinator

SIMON BÉRIDOT
IT Technician

YVES BABINEAU
Executive Chef – Craft Services

ANIK DE CARUFEL
Chef – Main Kitchen

FRANCIS BEAUVAIS
Sous-Chef – Main Kitchen
and Rendez-Vous Lounge

RICHARD SILVA
Sous-Chef – Rendez-Vous Lounge

Conclusion

History has revealed that the horse is a universal symbol, having inspired all cultures around the world. What is more, the horse has always been a muse for creators. Since humanity's evolution rests on the visions dreamed up by those who reimagine the world, I see *Odysseo* as a majestic work of art that builds bridges between all nations and elevates human nature. This show is as much a privilege and a pleasure to watch as it is to take part in.

If it is true that humanity's history only truly began when humans tamed the horse, in *Odysseo*, the horse has become the main star, without whom the show could not exist. It is because humans cared for the horse's well-being that they earned the animal's trust and friendship. Partners onstage and off, together they can win over any audience.

By taking us on a voyage between dream and reality, here and abroad, now and infinity, *Odysseo* is not only a tribute to the beauty of nature and the equine species, but also a triumph of the creative imagination of all those who worked together to bring us this one-of-a-kind show.

Before becoming a reality on stage, *Odysseo* was but the dream of a visionary artist who uses his creative genius to reinvent the equestrian arts and the performance arts. Today, a marvelous dream come true, *Odysseo* is a show that sows happiness wherever it goes. Odysseo's avant-garde designer and subtle art director, Normand Latourelle, melded the most innovative technological efficiency to the poetry of images, movement and sound to create this stunningly memorable adventure and veritable work of art. He took on the mission of creating a sense of well-being in the audience goers by demonstrating the symbiosis between humans and horses. According to almost all the spectators and members of the media who have seen *Odysseo* were amazed by it and plan to see it again, this is surely one of the most beautiful shows on our blue planet. We have to believe Normand Latourelle when he says, "If your belief and vision are unshakable and your perseverance unmovable, then success is inevitable."

Table of contents

Photo and illustration credits

ACMÉ: pages 104 and 110.

FRANÇOIS BERGERON: pages 32, 45, 63, 68-69, 112-113 and 174.

BERNARD BRAULT – *La Presse*: page 129.

IVANOH DEMERS – *La Presse*: page 130.

ÉLISE GENEST: endpaper.

GEODEZIK: pages 6-7 and 143.

LYNNE GLAZER: pages 39, 40-41, 48-49, 75, 95, 100, 101, 108, 109, 120, 121, 122, 124, 131 and 163.

MICHÈLE HAMEL and GEORGES LÉVESQUE: page 149.

SOPHIE LAUGHERA: pages. 114-115, 124, 141, 145, 150, 155, 157, 160, 161 and 162.

JEAN-FRANÇOIS LEBLANC: back cover page, pages 19, 21 and 58-59.

ALEXANDRE LEGAULT-DERY: pages 78, 116-117, 136, 138, 139, 152, 156, 170, 171 and 174.

ANDREW MILLER: page 125.

SHELLEY PAULSON: pages 9, 26-27, 28, 29, 30, 37, 42-43, 46, 51, 53, 54, 55, 56-57, 60, 61, 62, 64, 65, 66-67, 72-73, 74, 76, 83, 84, 88-89, 90, 118, 119, 120, 123, 141, 144, 146, 148, 149, 151, 161, 162 and 164.

PIFKO: page 4.

PASCAL RATTHÉ: cover page, pages 11, 13, 14-15, 17, 18, 22, 25, 31, 35, 47, 65, 70, 71, 74, 77, 79, 80-81, 85, 87, 91, 93, 94, 97, 98, 106-107, 119, 126, 128, 130, 132, 146, 147, 151, 165, 166, 167, 172 and 175.

ALBERT RUDNICKI: pages 127 and 140.

KERRY-JO STEWART: endpapers, pages 102-103, 104, 110, 111, 135 and 149.

The author would like to thank all the creative people, the artists and artisans and the department heads and managers who generously answered his questions. Their accounts make up the substance of this book.

EDITOR: Normand Latourelle

ASSOCIATE EDITOR: Jo-Anne Martin

ART DIRECTOR: Annie Reynaud

GRAPHICS: Multidisciplinary Team, with Tanya Paiva

TRANSLATION AND PROOFREADING: KG Traduction inc.

PROJECT COLLABORATORS: Louise Meilleur and Mélanie Ruel

Printed in Canada

Cavalia.net